D0927981

THE SLAVE
WHO BOUGHT
HIS FREEDOM

THE SLAVE WHO BOUGHT HIS FREEDOM

EQUIANO'S STORY
adapted by KAREN KENNERLY

DISCARD PUBLIC LIBRARY ASSOCIATION EASTHAMPTON

A Richard W. Baron Book

 E. P. DUTTON & CO., INC. NEW YORK

Equiano's story was first published in 1789 as *The Interesting Narrative of the Life of Olaudah Equiano, or Gustavus Vassa, the African. Written by Himself.*

Adaptation copyright © 1971 by Karen Kennerly

All rights reserved. No part of this publication may be reproduced or transmitted in any form or by any means, electronic or mechanical, including photocopy, recording, or any information storage and retrieval system now known or to be invented, without permission in writing from the publisher, except by a reviewer who wishes to quote brief passages in connection with a review written for inclusion in a magazine, newspaper, or broadcast.

Published simultaneously in Canada by Clarke, Irwin & Company Limited, Toronto and Vancouver

SBN: 0-525-39455-9
Library of Congress Catalog Card Number: 70-108969
Printed in the U.S.A.
First Edition

Slavery—United States

Equiano.

Vassa, Gustavus

Blacks—Biography

Black Autobiographies is a series designed to bring back
to life in modern language a rich heritage of first-person
stories obscured too long by dust and the formal English
prose of the eighteenth and nineteenth centuries. The
original accounts were written by black men and women,
most of them ignored by history. They tell of slavery,
escape, kidnapping, bravery, suffering, triumph, war, and
everyday life in times long gone.

CONTENTS

1	An Ibo Childhood	11
2	African Slavery	19
3	The Middle Passage	31
4	Barbados	43
5	North to Virginia, East to England	49
6	War in the Mediterranean	57
7	The Island of Montserrat	63
8	Trading in the Islands	69
9	Philadelphia	77
10	Buying Freedom	83
11	Trouble in Georgia	87
12	Bahamas Shipwreck	91
13	Return to Europe	99
14	To Sea Again	107
15	Arctic Voyage	111
16	The Mosquito Shore	115

THE SLAVE
WHO BOUGHT
HIS FREEDOM

CHAPTER 1

An Ibo Childhood

I WAS BORN in Africa in the year 1745. My people called me Olaudah Equiano. In the Ibo language these are the words for *well spoken* and *leader*. But when I was almost twelve years old, a white man named me Gustavus Vassa, and that has been my name, slave and free, ever since.

It was in the valley of Essaka that I was born, shaded by the tall rubber trees and always green with new-growing things. Our valley was far from the coast of the Atlantic Ocean, and even many days' journey from the Niger River. I had never heard of white men or Europeans, nor of the sea. We were a province in the powerful kingdom of Benin, but that meant nothing to me. For we governed ourselves, and the only strangers I saw as a child were the *Oye-Eboe*, which means *red men who live far away*. They are large people with skin the color of mahogany wood. They came from the Niger River to trade at

11

our markets and to buy slaves. Although I knew that only criminals and prisoners of war were sold as slaves, still I was afraid of these amber men. They always carried large sacks.

Because we were a gentle people living in a fertile valley, we needed only a simple form of government. Each village was ruled by several chiefs, or elders. My father was one of them. His greatness was marked by a scar of honor drawn straight across his forehead and down to the outer tips of his eyebrows. It looked like some magical bow to me. I had seen one of my five brothers marked in this way, and my mother used to say to me many times, "Olaudah, when you become the proper age, you too will have the bow drawn across your forehead."

When a crime had been committed, it was the elders who decided upon the punishment to be given. A kidnapper most frequently had to give up the person he had captured, as well as forfeit one of his own slaves. And if the theft was considered very serious, the thief himself would be condemned to slavery. But the worst crime of all, in the minds of my people, was adultery. The women found guilty of this were often put to death, though each case was judged separately: I remember one such woman who was spared because she was feeding a newborn baby from her breast.

Our style of life was simple. Each household made its own clay pots, and spun its own cloth, which was then dyed an indigo blue—the favorite color of the entire village. This brilliant blue was pressed from the leaves of some tree, and I've never seen a color quite like it in any European country. Men and women alike wrapped the cloth loosely around their bodies, and when there was a breeze, it swung slightly as they walked. Wives of elders, women like my mother, also wore gold bands on their arms and legs.

Men, women, and older children cultivated the rich land that lay beyond the village walls. Sometimes the land that had to be tilled was an hour's walk away, and all the villagers would set out together in the early morning. Since I was too young to go, I would watch them from a tree. It was beautiful to see the wind blow the blue cloth around their feet as they walked past the different color greens of pineapple plants, Indian corn, and tobacco leaves.

Some days, instead of working in the field, my mother would go to the market, and I would go with her. It was then that I saw the *Oye-Eboe* and heard their tales of Benin, which I could not fully understand. They brought us guns and dried fish. The fish pleased us the most, since our only waters were narrow brooks and springs. And because we were not really a warring nation. In exchange we gave them sweet-smelling woods and perfume made from a special kind of earth mixed with palm oil. They also valued our wood salt. This we got by burning mangrove bushes in large brass pans until nothing was left but a salty ash.

In the evenings, my mother would weave and bake in her house, while my father received friends in his. The "houses" of village elders were really many houses with a wall around. The wall was made of red earth baked hard by the sun. Each house had a high, thatched roof which pushed away the sun's heat. Some houses were open on all sides to let the breeze blow in on us; others had walls plastered smooth with a special mud that scared away insects while we were sleeping. Inside, the furniture was simple. We sat on smooth, cool logs, or on perfumed benches. Our beds were low and wide, made from the soft bark of banana trees.

My mother and father each had a day house and a night house. My father's day house stood in the exact center of the compound, and was divided into two rooms: in one he sat with his family and in the other he visited with friends. In his night house he slept with his sons. Except for me. I slept next door in the night house of my mother because I was her favorite. Other houses scattered within the compound were for our slaves. Every elder had many slaves, but they were treated with such respect that the word "slave" meant something very different to us than it does to Europeans.

For us, slaves became slaves by chance, not by birth. That is, they were most often prisoners of war. Instead of locking them up in prisons, we made them our servants. I said before that we were not a warring people. But occasionally we would have disputes with neighboring tribes, or suddenly be attacked by one of them. The fighting never took place within the village, but in the fields beyond the village walls. And when we had to fight, we fought well. For men and women alike were trained to use guns, bows and arrows, double-edged swords, spears. We were covered, neck to toe, front and back, by great painted shields. If we were victorious, we brought home all our captives and turned them into slaves, all but one. That was the chief of the enemy, who we killed.

The purpose of these small wars was not to gain new territory; it was simply to obtain prisoners. I now realize that the disputes must have been started by disloyal chiefs who secretly were slave-traders. For once a man became a slave, he could be sold— to the *Oye-Eboe*.

Of course, many slaves were not sold. These lived within family compounds and led lives much like ours. They did no more work than their masters, and always had the chance of becoming freemen again. I knew two slaves who actually rose to kingship.

Most of all, we loved to dance. We celebrated everything: triumphant return from war, harvest of the crops, weddings, offerings made to heaven, the day the sun crossed over the equator (our New Year). I cannot recall each holiday clearly. But in my memory is a sweet jumble of drums of different sounds, huge rattles, xylophones, and guitars. The dances themselves were always split into four groups. In the first, only married men danced. They acted out scenes from recent battles. The second group was made up of married women, who, with soft arms and slow steps, depicted recent family events. Then young men danced imitations of hunting, and the young girls pretended to be harvesting. As soon as one group finished its dance, another would begin—they seemed to go on in endless circles. Watching for a long time gave me a delicious feeling of dizziness.

My people believed that there is one god—we called him Chukwu—who lives in the sun and wears a great belt. He neither eats nor drinks, for he is superhuman and does not have such ordinary needs. But he does smoke a pipe, which for us is the greatest luxury of all. Chukwu determined the important events in our lives—if we should be captured and when we should die. But since there was no heaven or hell to us, he cared little for our afterlife. Dead relatives became the spirits that protected us. We offered to them food and drink, much in the same way a Catholic might light a candle for a favorite saint.

My mother felt particularly close to the spirit of her mother—who died before I was born—and on certain nights I would go with her to the tomb. It was in a small house away from all the others, and so dark at night that I could only dimly see my mother's bright clothes. She offered the food, and began a crying and a moaning which she did not quiet until dawn. Night birds hooted as if in answer, and they frightened me so much that I clung to my mother's bent back the whole time—though I was also a little afraid of her.

Then, when the sky became gray with early morning, my mother bathed herself, and bathed me, before returning home. For cleanliness at all times was the strictest law of our religion. And like the Jews, we had many ritual washings. Even at every meal, we first washed our hands, then offered a bit of food to the protective spirits before we ourselves could eat.

Although we had no temples, we did have priests, or wise men, whose main duty was to foretell events and read strange omens. Once a peculiar thing happened to me: I was standing in the middle of a road, when a poisonous snake suddenly crossed by, sliding between my legs without even flicking its sharp head at my calf. As if he *knew* me. The wise men told all my people that this meant I would be a great leader one day. But there was no chance for that to happen.

CHAPTER 2

African Slavery

WHEN THE GROWN-UPS went into the fields each day, the village was left empty and unprotected. So all the children stayed together within the walls of one family compound. We would take turns climbing a "lookout" tree to see if any strangers or large animals had entered the narrow avenues between the compounds. It was a game, really, like playing with the too-heavy spears that would wobble and fall in the dust when we tried to lift them above our heads. But one day I actually spotted a stranger, climbing over the wall of the very compound in which we were playing. He dropped to the ground, and I yelled; the children piled on top of him, while the oldest brought many ropes, and bound him up like a package. We never knew what happened to him after he was taken away that evening.

Some months later, Owi and I were left alone in our house. Owi was my only sister, a year younger than I, and we were always together. I played gentle games with her when other boys weren't about—I forgot about being a mock-warrior. On this particular day, we were sitting together on the hot sand and drawing pictures in the space between our knees. Then, so quick and horrible, we were dragged apart by heavy red hands. My feet lifted off the ground, and the last thing I saw was our drawing which looked small and silly from this new height. My mouth wrapped tight, I was stuffed into a sack. The same thing was happening to Owi. I got dizzy from being bounced in different ways. Whoever was carrying me must have been running, then climbing —back over my father's wall—then running again.

Evening came, and we were put down at a small house where robbers rest for the night. I was nearly sick from the smell of dried fish and perfume inside the sack. So they untied us. We saw then for certain that we were prisoners of *Oye-Eboe*—two men and a woman. Owi stared at them for a long time. She was almost calm in her curiosity. Then all at once she crumpled against me, and cried and cried. I think she realized for the first time that we were to be sold as slaves. Whispering plans of possible escape which we did not really believe, we went to sleep.

Another day and more traveling. Now we were allowed to walk, and the forests seemed different from those around our village. But then we came to a road which I thought I'd been on before. I saw people in the distance, and yelped for recognition.

But my face was pressed in the dirt of the road, and I was thrown back into the sack.

The second morning I was awakened by a sharp crying from my sister. One of the men was pulling her up. I got up too, quickly, but was thrown down again by the second man, who said, "Only her." And Owi disappeared.

Those words left me so numb with grieving that for days after that—I'm not sure how many—I didn't know what was happening to me. My hands were tied most of the time and my feet, too, when I wasn't walking. I wouldn't eat, and finally food was forced into my mouth. I was passed from hand to hand. I had become a slave. Among black people.

My first African master was a chieftain and a blacksmith. It was my job to work the bellows for his fire. As my elbows pumped in and out, making the flame grow bright, he pulled lumps of soft yellow gold into thin bands and fine ornaments. Like many chiefs, he had two wives. One of them was a little like my mother. She was good to me, and I spent much of the day playing with her children. Still, I was a slave and could not eat at their table. My natural pride wouldn't accept this, and so I plotted my escape.

After a month, my master trusted me enough to

let me roam about in the village. By this time I'd learned much about the roads and the location of my village. In a few more weeks, I'd have been ready to attempt my escape. But then something happened which destroyed my plans.

I was feeding the chickens one morning, and tossing pebbles up in the air while watching them eat, when one pebble came down on a chicken's outstretched neck, and killed it. I told the cook what happened. Enraged, she said the master should give me a beating, and went off to find him. Not used to being beaten, I ran off wildly into the forest. The bushes I hid beneath were quite close to the house, but so dense that no one could possibly see me. Someone called my name. Then I heard the rustle of many people gathered together, and a daylong village search for a missing slave began. Often people came so close to where I lay I could hear bits of conversation: "Stupid child—if he thinks he'll make it home—tigers and snakes won't give him a chance—thought of running away myself, but wouldn't last four hours out here at night—the spirits alone are enough to—" Evening came, and they went back home. Rustling leaves now suggested snakes to me instead of wind. I had given up the desire to escape; my master's house was "home" to me.

When the house was all asleep, I crept back into the shed that was the kitchen, and went to sleep on the ashes of the cook's fire. I dreamed I was on the forest floor, rolling this way and that to hide from the animals. All the monkeys of West Africa were after me: black monkeys with long tails, white-nosed monkeys, monkeys with beards and three stripes on their foreheads, monkeys with white cheeks and red crowns. Then I heard a jackal shriek—I woke up. It was the cook. She had come to light the morning fire and found me where I had been rolling in the ashes. I was as white as a bad spirit.

My master only scolded me, and ordered the others not to mistreat me.

The daughter of my master became ill with the fever. Medicine men were called in from the village; then others from distant villages. But the fever mounted and mounted, and she died. She had been my master's only daughter, and his grief became a sort of madness. He tried to kill himself many times. After a while, he stopped trying, but he did no work. I was sold.

It was a long time between masters, on the road with traders. The roads had become wider and smoother and the rest houses more frequent. I noticed other slavers now, with their captives, coming from different directions but going in ours. Our common road led us always west of the sun; beyond that, I comprehended nothing.

Coming toward us from a branch road there was a slaver with a long line of slaves. One behind the other, they were so closely and evenly spaced, I found it strange. They crossed onto our road. I saw that they were joined together by short leashes fastened to braids of leather that yoked their necks like oxen. Each carried some load on his head, like a bundle of corn or an elephant's tusk. Light and free, we easily passed them. My eyes snapped from face to face—the way you see houses on the shore from a fast-moving boat—when I stopped and froze. Owi's face! We clung to each other tight as two frightened bats in the blazing sunlight. I was vaguely aware of a soft rustling sound at our feet, which must have been the bundle of corn and grasses slipping off Owi's head. I also heard the dull thud of bodies bumping against bodies. For we had stopped the movement of the entire coffle (as I later learned such a roped line of slaves was called) . At first we couldn't speak, or even cry. But when we did begin to cry, we couldn't be stopped. All the while I was saying, "Where have you been? What country? Are you all right? Why are you tied by the neck, why are you tied—" Owi answered nothing, she only shook her head. Of course, how could she know?

Even the slavers were saddened by our meeting, and loosened Owi from her collar so we could spend that one night together. We lay on either side of my owner. We held hands across his chest and did not sleep all night. Those few, dark hours were the happiest I'd had in months. But the next morning she was dragged away from me once more. I never saw her again.

I was put up for sale in the beautiful town of Tinmah. We walked beneath the shade of tall trees to reach the town square: instead of being the usual dusty marketplace, it was one, large, shimmering pond. The brightness of the sunlight playing on this great mirror of water dazzled me. People were bathing there. They would slide into the pond waist deep, their skirts growing heavy and rippled under the water's surface. With jugs made of brass, they scooped up the water and poured it in wet streams onto their necks and backs. It was splendid to watch— this dipping into the pond, then pouring, dipping, and pouring.

"I'll buy him. What is his price?"

"One hundred and seventy."

I looked away from the pond, startled, and down at the two shadows near my feet. A woman was talking with my owner. I looked up at her slowly. On her arm were wide bracelets made of ivory; bracelets so white and wide that whole figures of warriors were finely carved on them. She held in her other hand a pouch from which she poured many little white shells the size of a fingernail. She counted out 170 of them and gave them to the slaver. These shells were the currency of whatever province I was in. She and I went off, away from the pond and toward the trees where the village houses poked through the leaves like tree houses. The sound of rushing water seemed all around me. Then I noticed that everywhere little rivers poured out of the woods and into the pond.

The woman's shaded house stood between two streams, and wide porches extended over them like high bridges. On the porch, beyond where we stood, was a small beast. The size of a cat and spotted like a leopard, it sat on its haunches as if ready to spring; but it remained motionless. Its coat was peculiarly smooth—perhaps wet from swimming in the stream. The sun, flickering on and off through the treetops, now lit on this creature for a second. I saw it was made of bronze! My mistress, who had been watching me, took me over to the statue and told me that it came from the capital of Benin, which was famous for its bronze and ivory sculpture. Even up close, the expression in its face and the roundness of its body were completely lifelike. My mistress went on to tell me that her husband had been to Benin several times, and had brought back many beautiful objects. I thought, "So, I'm to work for a blacksmith again," but she added: "He died five years ago. And my son needs a companion. I think you will like each other."

I was taken away by servants who bathed and perfumed me. That evening they led me into a room where a table was spread with foods I hadn't seen before, like coconuts and sugarcane. Across from me sat a boy about my age. I didn't know what was expected of me, or why I, a slave, was to eat alongside of a rich freeman's son.

"How old are you?" he asked.

"Eleven, and a few months."

"I'm just past ten. You must start first."

It was the custom in our land for the eldest at the table to begin eating before the others can do so.

It took me no time at all to act like a freeman again. For although I was still a slave, my new friend and his beautiful mother did not treat me like one. Despite the great distance I must have been from my village, our languages were much alike, and we could easily understand one another. We played all day, running to the bright sun over the pond and back into the woods, pretending to be warriors.

My companion showed me his other treasures from Benin. The one most mysterious to me was a tiny ivory mask, which his father had worn as a belt buckle. The carved face was noble, yet tender. I thought of it as a portrait of his father, and looked at it for long periods of time. I was completely happy.

One morning, before the sun was up, I was awakened and hurried away from my sleeping companion. I never learned why I was sold.

Walking again, west of the sun. But no longer through an Africa I recognized. It was the hell of Africa. People never washed before eating, they cooked bad-smelling meats in iron pots. They fought among themselves with their fists. Their teeth were filed to sharp points. Ornamental scars slashed across their bodies. I was thrown among them, and couldn't speak their language.

At last we came to the bank of a large river. Knowing only ponds and streams before this, I was astonished. I could barely see the opposite shore, and that panicked me. People actually lived on this river, in canoes big enough to hold all their belongings. I was put into one of these canoes, and was paddled through wet, hot country. Mud was everywhere. On both sides were mangrove trees fifty feet high. Their roots grew straight up from the mud, thick and twisting as the snakes that lived in these swamps. The air was filled with mosquitoes. Crocodiles swam near our boat, their eyes and teeth breaking the surface of the water. At night, the canoes would go next to the shore and each family would build a fire. Some slept on the boats; others slept on shore, in tents made from grass mats which they carried with them in the boats. Day after day we moved through the water. Sometimes we passed burned and empty villages. Later I learned those villages had been attacked by black warriors, who then sold the people living there to traders.

The river widened, and our journey ended at a small mud island with shacks built on it. Other slaves had been brought there, and all of us were waiting. I didn't know for what. But we waited, two, three days. On the third day, two giant canoes came for us. They were sixty or seventy feet long and seven feet across. Each one was paddled by about forty men, and, in each, there were as many as twenty warriors carrying guns. Strapped to the front of each canoe was a small brass cannon. We had been waiting for a slave fair to take place, I soon learned. All day the auctioning went on, our owners and the traders quarreling over what price each of us was worth. We were exchanged for rum, ammunition, and tobacco. At the end of the day, those who had brought us to the island left. The next morning we were packed into the large canoes. On the bottom lay slaves already bought, bound and tied. We headed downriver. The water got wider and wider, until the land to the left fell out of sight.

Eight or nine months after being kidnapped, I had arrived at the seacoast.

CHAPTER 3

The Middle Passage

I HAD NEVER seen anything so flat as the sea, nor so tall and upright as the slave ship sitting on the edge of the sea. Surely we had been brought to some world of the bad spirits, and the spirits themselves lived inside that high boat. The river water was running fast now, and our canoe with it. At the place where the river melted into the ocean, the water rocked violently. Several men were hanging over the side of the canoe. We left the mouth of the river and I heard a huge sound—a *thrump-wish* that echoed like a thousand drums. It was the ocean banging against the white, thin edge of the land which made this drumming. Other canoes like ours were moving in the same direction. These long boats looked like so many fishing lines being pulled in by the great ship. Sharks swam near our boat. Three or four slaves tried to jump out to them, for they preferred being eaten by fish in the sea to meeting with spirits. But the traders wouldn't let them go. I looked back at the length of white sand and saw a rebellious slave lying flat, clutching handfuls of sand in an attempt to remain on Africa.

Our boat slid over sudden dark water, and the ship was in front of us. It rose up in decorated layers: planks jointed together; then windows; brass guns jutting from holes; more planks. Standing straight on the ship's flat top were several of the longest poles I'd ever seen—so long I couldn't imagine what sort of tree's trunk had been used for them. Smaller poles crossed these at different heights. An uncountable number of ropes fell from the tall poles onto the ship like a tangle of jungle vine. I feared we were expected to get caught in them, as a kind of trap. But most frightening were the squares of white tied to the cross-poles, because I couldn't possibly figure out why they were there, or even what they were. From a distance and against the sunlight, they had looked like birds' wings. But up close they were ugly. They either battered and flapped against the poles, or hung limp and dirty. Perhaps they were bad clouds that fell from the sky and now waited, like vultures, above us. And maybe they caused the terrible smell coming from the ship.

A long plank lowered from the ship and hooked onto our canoe. The naked slaves (we had all been stripped of our clothing by now) had to walk up it two by two. Each pair was padlocked together by iron rings. One set of rings bound the right wrist of one slave to the left of the other; another set bound the ankles in the same way. Women also were joined together like this. Because there were few children as young as myself, we were handed up, and for a moment I got the same feeling I had had when I was lifted into the air by these *Oye-Eboe* who first captured me.

They put me down "on deck." Men with skin a color I'd never seen before tossed me up and poked me, apparently to see if I was healthy. They joked about me in a language made of sounds I'd never heard. Then they let me stand free on the oily floor. At the other side was a huge copper pot, boiling. And all around, in rows, black people of every description. I recalled bits of talk about the "ship-men" being cannibals. (I had never met cannibals anywhere in Africa and had believed that talk of such people was made up.) The faces of these Africans were so pained and miserable that I suddenly believed what I had heard, and fainted.

When I woke, some black traders were teasing me, trying to cheer me up. I wouldn't play with them; I only asked if I were going to be eaten by those white men with horrible looks, red faces, and loose hair. They laughed hard, repeating it to one another as if it were a joke, and said: "Who would pay such a big price for such a small dinner?" A white man wanted me to drink a kind of liquor from a glass, but I wouldn't touch his hand. A black man took it from him and gave it to me. The drink, instead of making me calm, upset me even more by the strange feeling it sent through my body. Soon after, the black man who gave me the glass returned to shore, and I felt completely alone.

Until then, I had been most afraid of the kind of horrible things that I knew happened to some people —like being a slave or being taken away by evil African spirits. But now I was afraid of horrors I didn't know. If these hideous people were spirits, why didn't they look like the bad spirits described to me at home? No one had told me spirits lived in hollow places on the water. No one had even told me about waters so large they never ended. And why were we here if not to be eaten? Why did they make us live in such filthy places below the deck and yet want us to stay alive—so much so that they would hold our mouths open by iron clamps and force food into our throats if we refused to eat? I could figure out nothing. Living that way, day after day, was like learning to live all over again, as if I were a baby.

Our ship did not move for many weeks, although other ships like ours did: one came out of the distance, closer and closer to us. The cloth on its cross-poles really did look beautiful—stretched, and rounded, and white. Then the people on the ship threw out a very heavy thing that splashed down through the water, and at once the ship stopped. I heard some black people talk about magic. White people called it an anchor. The masters on that boat seemed very happy to see those on ours, and came aboard to drink liquor with them. They must have known one another before. I was now very puzzled and asked a black man who came from my country about them:

"Do they have a country besides these hollow floating ones?" They did, but it was very far away. "Then," I said, "why did no one in our country hear of it?" Because it is too distant to have known about. "Do they have women that look like themselves?" I kept on. They did. "Why, then, don't we see them?" Because they were left behind in their country. "How does the boat move back to that country?" This he couldn't answer. Possibly the white men put some spell on the water when they wanted to go and to stop; it had something to do with the ropes and pieces of white cloth. Then I asked him again if we were to be eaten, and my fears about this were finally stopped when he said no, that we were being carried to their country to do work for them. Some blacks must have known this before they were brought on board. For I was amazed to see them totally unafraid of white men. They examined their chalky skin and felt the hair on their heads to see if it was securely fastened to the scalp. After a black was satisfied with his inspection, he would laugh at this ridiculous being.

While we stayed in one place, more slaves were being brought on the boat, and I was allowed to go free on the deck. Some black men boasted among themselves about rebelling—very few white men could understand any of our languages—but there were armed soldiers by all the railings, and no one on our ship dared. It had happened, on some ships, and had worked: all the white men had been killed. But then, so had most of the blacks.

Finally the ship was getting ready to move, and talk

of rebellion stopped. For "sailing" was white man's magic, and the black men felt more defeated by that than by the men themselves. I myself was excited that we were going to leave, because I wanted to see how they did it. But I was thrown into the terrible hole beneath the deck and saw nothing.

This was where the slaves on ship lived. It was, simply, a hole—or a series of holes, one for men, another for women, a third for women very pregnant or with small babies. Each hole was just a little higher than myself, so a grown-up had to stoop to enter. Shelves built all along the sides divided this space into shallow halves. The floor and shelves were nailed with rough boards; nothing at all lay over them. Indeed, there was nothing else in this space except people; there was no room. Black people covered the floors and platforms. There wasn't even space for a person to turn around, and they had to remain day and night in a sleeping position, with the knees of one tucked into the back of another. Their elbows rubbed constantly against the boards. Even here, they were chained together. When one had to relieve himself—which meant going to a huge waste-barrel in the middle—he had to drag his chained partner with him, ankle cuffs clanging together as they stepped across the other bodies. Children often fell into these disgusting tubs, and many got sick from the odor alone. When I was first taken aboard, they tried to make me stay in this room. But I fainted again and so, because of my age, they let me stay on deck. But now it was time to "set sail," and they had more to care about than whether I lived or died.

Because I thought this, when they put me in the "hold," I stopped caring also. Waiting for death was, in a grim way, exciting. My body was numb and tingly from lying even more still than I had to in the flat, locked line of men. The pressure of two bodies, front and back, drained me. I was not conscious of being squeezed by them; rather, I was melting away, while they were slowly filling the space I occupied. Terror left me, and I felt a kind of total peacefulness. I listened to the rolling moans of the slaves, counter-rhythmed by sharp points of sound from the deck: an order shouted to a sailor; the quick pulling on ropes; running feet. I heard it all as if it had nothing to do with me. I didn't move for days.

I must have been half-dead when they found me (or "found me out." They considered it bad behavior when a slave wanted to die). A white sailor shook me, tried to make me stand, and finally carried me up on deck.

I was left unchained in the open air for the rest of the journey. It was odd, being small, and on deck, while the others were below in the holds. I felt like a sailor who climbs up a "mast" and stays for long hours in a kind of eagle's nest, watching. A few slaves were with me on deck—the prettiest of the women. White men called them Black Venus, and they were allowed to go free so the sailors could touch them. If a "Venus" once refused, or even showed displeasure, she would be punished. I saw one woman strapped naked across a barrel-like thing with handles at either end that they used for winding up ropes. I noticed a brand burned into her left buttock. It was set like a deep shadow in the sunny, smooth surface of her behind. A red bandana—a sailor's gift for a time when she had submitted—was knotted around her waist, its ends fluttering pitifully with the breeze. Then they beat her. She would not moan at all, but the expression on her still face afterward made me more sad than all the sounds of pain that came from below deck in the hold. One day while this was happening, I had a sudden fright for my mother. (Up until then I'd imagined her as living her unchanging life.) Perhaps my whole family had been captured and my mother forced on deck to be a "Venus." I cried uncontrollably, and the sailors, mistaking the reason, made ugly gestures about my being in love with the woman they'd whipped.

When the sky was clear and the sea quiet, the slaves were brought up for exercise and chained to the deck railings. They were told to be "happy" because it was time to "dance." One slave drummed on an upturned kettle, a sailor blew away on his bagpipes, and we danced. Those who were chained hung their arms limp in front of their bellies and hopped from one foot to the other, ankle links clanging in a rhythm different from that of the drum. Unbound slaves had to dance all around the deck, in and out of the chained line as the sailors clapped and hooted. They laughed sometimes when I'd slip where blood from the slaves' bruised ankles wetted the deck. The sailors clapped faster, shouted at us to be happier, to sing. And we'd sing. Out of tune, in different languages, we all sang songs of great sadness. It wasn't tribal music as the sailors thought, but ship music. Songs that none of us knew before or had ever sung in Africa.

While most of us were dancing in the fresh air, some had to clean out the holds. The floor would be covered with blood: the empty rooms were shiny red and bad-smelling. And there was never time to mop a room thoroughly before the slaves came back. Week after week it got worse as more became sick.

At least one-third of the slaves died. Every day before our morning meal of stewed yams and half a pint of water, a ship's doctor inspected the slaves. When he found one who had died during the night, he unlinked him from the ankle of his "partner," hooked the live man up to someone else, and had the body taken on deck. All the bodies were piled in a heap, which the sailors then threw overboard. A minute later the arched backs of sharks cut above the water. Then they too went under. These were the same sharks that followed the ship from Africa.

Death was better than slavery for a lot of us. We even believed that, once drowned, a man would return to his village and family. The sailors kept a constant watch-out for suicides. But, despite their caution and despite threats of severe beatings, many tried and some succeeded. Two men from my country were on deck one day when the nets—usually bunched tight against the side of the ship—were left hanging loose after some garbage had been spilled over the railing. The men saw the ocean sparkle in through the gap between the ship and the blown-out net, and they jumped into it. A third man tried to follow them a few seconds later. But the wind had slapped the nets back against the ship's side, and he leapt like an open-mouthed fish straight into the netting. He had the look of someone gone blind, as his arms and legs poked against the strings in ridiculous directions. Horribly fascinated, I was unable to move, until a rush of sailors pushed me away. They gathered in the net and flopped the man back onto the deck. Alarm bells rang across the ship. It stopped moving. A group of sailors lowered a small boat down to the water and began to row fast toward the two heads that were still bobbing above the green. But before they reached them, the men waved their arms like happy madmen, and went under. The man who had not made it was whipped almost to death. I was more puzzled than ever by white men: always wanting to keep us alive and yet always ready to kill us.

Much of the whites' behavior was puzzling to me; such incidents frightened me more than when I myself was whipped hourly for not eating at the beginning of the voyage. For example, I saw one of their own men tied to a mast, then beaten so badly that he died from it. And they tossed him over the side as they would one of us. There was a day when they caught a great number of fish, more than they could possibly use. After they had eaten their fill, we begged them for the leftovers. "You eat only what's good enough for you," they said, and threw the fish over one by one, watching our faces and laughing.

But I ceased to be afraid of them, out of sheer curiosity. Since I was mostly alone on the deck and they seemed to tolerate me, I stood quite close to watch them tie knots and pull on ropes that changed the shapes of the sails. One small instrument used to take measurements of the sky fascinated me the most. I think my astonishment made one sailor a little proud, because he decided to show me how truly grand the instrument was by letting me look through it. I saw clouds large and heavy as land, with ponds and hills slanting sideways. They moved—sailed—quickly out of sight. But when I looked at the sky without the instrument, the clouds were flat white and unmoving. I still believed it was all a foreign magic.

CHAPTER 4

Barbados

THE SEA LOOKED like the same large, blue disk, but the sailors had changed. They seemed happy all of a sudden, chattery as if expecting something to happen. We were given more to eat and made to drink all the water we could, so our bellies would fill and swell. A day or so after this began, I saw that the circle of sky meeting ocean, which I had gotten used to, was broken at one point by a dim shape, also blue. I thought it was a storm cloud, and watched for it to break and smoke into the sky. But it remained tight and hard, hour after hour. Then a sailor who'd been looking through the instrument let out a hooray so loud that his voice nearly squeaked; the yell was carried from sailor to sailor, up and down the ship. They tried to make us understand how excited we should be—we were almost "there." I knew now it was land in the distance, but I didn't understand why I or any of us should be pleased. The fear of being eaten came back to me. Perhaps they'd simply been saving us to sell as provisions to their people.

Night, and morning again. Now we were close enough to the island of Barbados for me to see that their country was made of land familiar to me—hills of uneven height, trees, fields that lay on the other side of the beach. It was very green and very gentle. I felt comforted.

It was our last day at sea, and the sailors wanted a party. Those slaves in fairly good health were brought out of the hold and unchained. The sailors got drunk and danced their own jerky, stiff-legged little dances as the bagpiper played. In the center of the deck they heaped a pile of old ripped sailors' suits. "Costuming" was the climax of the party. The sailors fell into the pile, dragged out middy blouses, threw them at the women, and made large, sloppy gestures of dressing. Or one of them would bag a pretty woman himself—sliding the cloth across her blinded head. Finally the head reappeared, startled and black above the white middy. Dressed, they danced with the sailors in identical clothes and clashing rhythms.

The next morning, the sails were tied down, and we were drifting into the calm water where ships of all sizes sat waiting and empty. White flecks showing through the leaves of trees must have been their houses. People were gathering on the shore, some in pants of the sort I was now used to seeing, others in heavy skirts shaped like bells and in stiff, curling hats. I'd never seen people so completely covered with clothes. Some of the men boarded our ship from a small boat, and all the slaves were gathered on deck. These men were merchants. They made each of us jump up and down to see how much strength we had left; they bent us over and examined us for sickness. Wherever possible, we had been painted with brown-colored ointments to hide any traces of disease. Then the merchants divided us into groups and packed us back into the hold for one more night. The fear of being eaten was once more alive among all of us. Our pained and bitter crying must have been unpleasant for the white men to hear, because in the middle of the night they brought some old slaves from the island to calm us down. They told us we'd been brought here only to work, and that as soon as we were on land we would see more Africans than white men.

We tottered down the plank and went to shore in long boats. Indeed, Africans of all languages greeted us on the beach. I heard someone in the crowd speak a tongue something like mine, and this excited me. I pushed my way deeper among them, groping crazily for my own, exact dialect. But instantly I was noticed missing from my group, or "parcel," and thrown back with the frightened herd.

We were penned up in the merchant's yard, the lot of us constantly moving about, like hysterical sheep. Everything I saw shocked me. Houses—close up—were really two or three houses piled one on top of the other. Men rode the backs of thin-legged beasts that looked like antelopes or gazelles, only they were larger and seemed almost as intelligent as men. But a slave in the compound who came from a different part of Africa said they too had horses where he came from, and larger than the ones here.

Not much later, we were sold in a "scramble." The price for each parcel of us had already been agreed upon by the merchant and purchasers. At a loud cracking noise, the purchasers ran into the pen to get first choice of the parcel they wanted most. As we were claimed, we'd be tagged with bits of paper or have a kerchief tied to our wrists. We were led out, away from the others. Only then did we understand why we had been grouped in parcels. No concern had been given to putting members of the same family in one parcel. Now brothers, husbands, and wives knew they wouldn't see each other again. The panic was more shrill and intense than that in the hold the night before we landed. I thought again of Owi.

Changes now came so quickly that I remember movement, sounds, colors, but few details. My parcel had been bought by a plantation owner, but right before he was to take us inland, he decided I was too small to work well, and he sold me to an auctioneer. With other leftovers—most of them sick or crippled—I marched in a ragged slave parade, led by a sailor playing bagpipes. Up and down the public square we went, and buyers smoking in front of shops looked us over. That evening was the auction. Inside a rum-smelling tavern, standing in front of a bright candle, we were sold one by one. Men from dark tables shouted numbers on top of numbers. The auctioneer would repeat the last number and wait for a higher one, his eyes always on the burning candle. When the candle had burned down the length of my thumb, he would shout "sold!" and begin again with the next slave. I was never sure of who the man was that bought me; but I was back in some merchant's pen, then on another ship—bound for North America.

CHAPTER 5

North to Virginia, East to England

THE COAST OF North America was endless, and I began to know that some countries—like Barbados—were smaller than the ocean while others—like Africa and America—were larger. Day after day, strips of beach or stiff, dark trees appeared and disappeared, until at the place called Virginia County the ocean cut into the land, and we turned in with it. The river here was salty, deep, and quiet. From the high trees on either bank, cool air floated down in sheets on our decks. There were no villages or people living in canoes; for a time, there was no one at all. Few slaves came with me on this voyage. We'd been fed well—plenty of rice and fat pork—and the whites hadn't bothered us.

We came to a port far up the river, and there we were taken ashore. I found very few Africans, and none who could speak with me. A handful of blacks were scattered out over a tobacco plantation. I picked stones and weeded grass for weeks. Occasionally during the day I saw a black head nod through distant leaves. Then, after a while, even they went away, and my loneliness was complete. I became totally absorbed in the muted sound of tearing grass, and in my wish to die.

The gentleman who owned the plantation was sick one day, and I was called in to fan him. The house was larger than any I'd ever seen, roofed porches flinging out in three directions. Empty chairs with high backs were grouped as if people were sitting in them. I went around the porches and entered through the kitchen. A black slave, who was cooking the dinner, wore an iron instrument that locked her head and muzzled her mouth so she could scarcely talk, and not eat at all. I went across the kitchen, into a room with a table large and shiny as a small pond, through other rooms, to my master. He was asleep, though his head made nervous little brushing strokes against the corner of his quilted chair. My guide moved me by my hips until I was in the exact proper spot. He folded my ten fingers around the long pole of a peacock-feather fan. Keeping his hands over mine, he moved my stiffened arms up and down. As the pole stroked the air, the brilliant feathers spread a little, bent back, curled under—like a bird not sure whether to fly off or skim the water. A few hairs on the top of my master's silver head lifted and fell as I fanned. My guide told me, good—do not stop. He left me alone in the room.

I dared to look around. A great watch hung on the opposite wall. As soon as I saw it, I was aware of the loud noise it made. Because it click-clocked, the same sound my tongue makes when clapping the roof of my mouth, I was afraid it would tell the gentleman anything I did wrong. Its face was beautifully painted with two sets of numbers and lines twirling in the corners. Every little while, one of its hands jumped—tock. When I turned my head a little more I saw a picture of a man who was looking at me. I knew it wasn't a window and a real man standing; it had to be some miraculous way of preserving dead spirits. He stood in a garden with a pretty slave ship fluttering far behind him. His suit was glossy black, and his stockings were white. One hand was in his pocket. The other hung over a rock on which his elbow was resting. The fingers were long and white and held—as if they would let it drop any moment—a carved stick. The eyes never stopped looking, and the stick never fell. I had worked myself into a state of terror, when finally my master woke, and sent me away.

A man named Michael Henry Pascal came from London to visit my master. He was a merchant, and stayed in my master's house while his ship's holds were being stacked with Virginia tobacco. He seemed to like me, and said he wanted to make a gift of me to some friends in England, was willing to pay as much as thirty or forty pounds sterling—I forget which. I was sold.

When his ship was ready to sail, I went to the

harbor on horseback led by an old slave who walked in front. This type of travel was very odd to me: I could have walked, and just as fast—instead I was rocking forward, high off the ground, my legs barely able to cup the horse's warm, silky belly. But I could see marvelous distances that the bushes and low trees usually hid from me.

The *Industrious Bee*—as the ship was called—was still wet from washed decks, and smelled of her sweet cargo. I was the only slave aboard, but I had a pile of sails to sleep on and plenty of good food to eat. Besides, I was beginning to understand English.

My American master had named me Jacob. The captain decided I should be called Gustavus Vassa, but I refused it, telling him as best I could that I already had a name and that it was Jacob. He insisted. I was stubborn and pretended not to hear when he called me Gustavus until I'd been slapped many times. Finally, I gave in, and have lived with the name of that early Swedish king ever since.

As I could now speak a little English, I mumbled out all the questions I'd wanted to ask since my first voyage. The sailors couldn't resist teasing me, and gave me absurd answers. I believed them all. One day they told me we were headed back to Africa; the next, to a strange country where everything was white and the sea turned hard as glass. Or they would talk loudly among themselves about whether I would taste good, until I was trembling with fear—then turn to me abruptly and say, "Don't they eat people in your country? They do in ours." I'd shout No! and run and hide in some little room, where my friend Dick would find me and comfort me.

Dick's full name was Richard Baker. He was four years older than I, a native of America but educated in England. Although he had many slaves, he never treated me like one. He was my first and closest white friend: we hugged fast to each other on stormy nights and ate at the same table. He always understood my gestures and mixed-up sentences, so was able to correct me and interpret for me. The captain thought it was a great joke that Dick and I were friends and used to tease me by saying he'd decided to eat Dick instead. This frightened me nearly as much as the thought of my own death. One night the sea raged so that a sailor was swirled overboard and drowned. I thought the captain had done something to anger the sea, and feared that Dick or I would be thrown into it to make it calm down again.

We weren't, and I worried that the sea would remember that and bear a grudge. One day, a group of whales came toward our ship. In the morning they were pale gray shapes bobbing like buoys between the ocean and haze; by evening they were the largest fish I'd ever seen, swimming so close to the ship that the fountains of water they shot from their heads splashed down on the deck. Dick said a whale could eat a man whole. Everyone was worried and the sailors began filling a barrel with wood tar. When it was dark, they lit the tar and threw the flaming barrel into the water. That must have been the offering the sea had been waiting for, because the whales swam toward where the torch sparked, and we never saw them again.

We docked at Falmouth, England, after thirteen weeks of rough sailing. I was then nearly twelve years old. The city confused me. It seemed a patchwork of wood and stone, where even the streets were not made of earth, and houses of various shapes pressed one next to the other. Every day Dick and I would leave the ship for a few hours. I memorized the crossings and recrossings of streets, studied shop windows, tried to understand the stone-cold hush and low mutterings of churches. One morning I woke to find the deck covered with white. I ran to tell the mate that someone had sifted salt over the entire ship during the night. He asked me to bring a handful to him. It was very cold, which surprised me. He told me to taste it. It had no taste at all, and he said it was snow. But try as he might, he could not make me understand what snow was. Later that afternoon, snow fell from the sky like rain, but dropping from a lower sky, and more gently. Dick explained the connection between snow and the god of these churches. Finally I understood that the English god was the maker of all things and very much like our sun god in Africa.

The captain, my master, went to stay with friends in Falmouth, and I went with him. They had a daughter, six or seven years old, and she grew very fond of me. When we were to leave, she cried and wouldn't stop until they promised that I would be left behind to play with her. But I—fearing this meant I'd have to marry her—was miserable until my master told me he would take me with him. In the middle of the night, we sneaked back to the ship, and sailed to the island of Guernsey, which lies between England and France.

There, Dick and I stayed with the family of the first mate. He had a daughter whom I liked very much, and his wife tended to me as she would her own child. In those quiet months, I learned from her and from Dick all about God, and enough of the English language to speak it quite well and understand everything. My main frustration was that I could not read. I had seen Dick sit for hours turning pages in a book. Once when he wasn't there, I lifted the book to my ear, hoping it would speak what it had to say since I couldn't read. But it was silent.

CHAPTER 6

War in the Mediterranean

I WAS BECOMING very English. Where, before I had feared everything, now I feared nothing—that in itself is very English. Things strange to me were funny customs to be learned. New adventures were simply stories waiting eagerly to be told when I'd return to London. The dangers of such ventures I left up to my new-found God.

Captain Pascal, still my master, placed me in the household of two unmarried sisters named Guerin. I waited on them, and they doted on me. Once again I was treated like a son. They sent me to school and decided I should be baptized. The captain was against the idea for reasons I wasn't to understand until three years later. But the kind women insisted, and in February, 1759, I was baptized *Gustavus Vassa* in St. Margaret's Church, Westminster, London. During those three years, I led two alternating lives that contrasted as dizzily as fireworks against a night sky. In one, I spent months fighting next to my master, who commanded a ship in the war against the French. In the other, I passed quiet, solemn hours, learning to read and write while living with the Guerins.

Almost six months after I was baptized, my master's ship sailed for the Mediterranean Sea. We anchored at Gibraltar on the southern tip of Spain, waiting. One day when I was on shore, a mate ran to me saying he'd found the sister I had told him of being separated from—he'd bring me to her. I felt almost sick with intensity. As I walked behind him, all my expectation gathered tight in my jaw. I was afraid. My main worry was that I wouldn't be able to speak at all. I saw her: my anxiety loosened and flowed down through my neck and arms—my mouth became so limber! But she turned, and it wasn't Owi. She did look quite a bit like her, and I tried politely to speak with her. But we weren't even from the same country.

Ships came and went while ours lay idle at Gibraltar. One, the *Preston,* was sailing home from Turkey, and my master told me Dick would be aboard her. I hadn't seen him for a year and a half. For hours, while the *Preston* was dropping her sails, I leaned out from the shore, expecting to see Dick the next minute, and then the next. Finally, the captain of the ship came on land and I ran to him—rudely, before he even reached my master—and asked, "My friend Dick, Richard Baker, when will he come on shore?" The captain answered that Richard Baker was dead.

I almost failed to understand him. It had been Dick who had explained the world of white men to me, who turned it into a reality I could be part of. Now that he was dead I wondered if there was any world for me at all. The ship's crew brought my master the sailor's chest that contained Dick's things, and he gave it to me. The sight of it broke through my shock, and I grieved for days. The chest and its contents I still have.

Not long after that, we fought the French fleet. Masts broad with all the sails they could crowd, we entered battle. We lay on the deck, our cheeks flat against the wet, salty wood. We listened for the sound of a cannon fired from an enemy ship and for its echo as it thudded into our ship's sides or splintered a cabin. Then our shot, and its echo. I snaked back and forth across the deck bringing powder to refill the guns. All around me people were torn into shreds by enemy guns. But for some reason I was never hurt. Afterward, we stuffed the holes in our ship with wax and strapped her sides together with thick ropes until we got back to some island where the ship would be properly repaired. There we waited for the next battle.

A gunner who was a heavy drinker had his cabin directly above mine. One night when we were rocking gently at sea and the war was at a dead calm, he suddenly woke from dream, babbling and shaking. He said St. Peter had warned him to repent because the life remaining to him was short. At four o'clock in the morning he lit candles and woke other seamen to give away his full supply of liquor. Still unable to sleep, he paced the floor of his cabin furiously, reading his Bible. At that moment, there were cries from the far deck and a shuddering that seemed as if the sea were quaking. In the black night, a ship had run broadside into us, her bow shattering the very bed where the gunner had been sleeping. He himself was only slightly hurt. Amid all the scurrying to save our ship, I thought of how I would tell this story to the Misses Guerin—how it would please them to see my belief in God confirmed.

We returned to England to have our ship repaired and refitted. On our way out again to the Mediterranean, we had to wait at the harbor of Portsmouth—none of us knew why. As we sat there for about a month, rumors of peace spread throughout the ship. Then one day victory was announced—absolute and official. We were ordered up to London where all of us would be paid off for our services. Such joyous and reckless plans we all made for celebration, and for the new lives we would begin! I had learned a great deal in the last year of the war. A clerk had taught me how to write, and the basic rules of arithmetic. Another man who waited on the captain showed me how to shave a man's beard and dress hair. He was about 40 years old, very well educated. We grew very close, talking deep into the night about the Bible and how much its teachings were like the beliefs and customs of my native village. He used to say that he and I would never part; that once we were paid, he would teach me his business and after a while we'd go into partnership together. We never questioned that my master would give me my freedom once we reached London.

Our ship sailed up the River Thames with the tide and anchored at high water. About half an hour after the tide turned and was pulling out toward the sea, my master ordered a long boat to be manned. He forced me into it without any warning, muttering: "You had plans to leave me—well, I'll take care you don't." His face was suddenly locked in a hardness I'd seen on many white faces, and at that moment he ceased to be "my good master." I became very calm. I asked for my books and chest. He swore, and said he wouldn't let me out of his sight. I answered that I was free by law to go get it. Raging so uncontrollably that I couldn't even understand his language, he leaped into the barge himself and ordered the rowers to head downriver. The whole crew was as astonished as I—the rowers were on the point of disobeying him until he swore at them as well. We passed ships readying to leave with the outgoing tide. As we did, my master shouted to each captain: Are you headed for the West Indies, and will you take on a slave? All the while I sat crumpled and broken. The rowers tried to cheer me up by talking of plans for smuggling me back to London. Once on English land, being a seaman and a baptized Christian, I would have certain rights which my master would have trouble ripping from me. But as long as I remained at sea, the captain of my ship was king and lawmaker.

A ship full-sailed and waiting to catch the tide was willing to take me on. She was the *Charming Sally* and heading for the island of Montserrat. Closeted in the cabin with my master and the strange captain, I was questioned. Captain Doran he was called. He asked me if I knew him. I answered no.

"Then," he said, "you are now my slave."

I told him my master could not sell me to him or to anyone else.

"Why," said he, "didn't your master buy you?"

I confessed he did. "I have served him for many years, and he has taken all my earnings made during the war except for one sixpence. And besides, I have been baptized. By English law, no man, therefore, has the right to sell me. I heard a lawyer tell my master that."

My old master—who had been silent—replied quietly, "That man was not your friend; he had confused one law with another and did not take the trouble to correct himself."

But I came back with, "It is very extraordinary that others do not know the law as well as you."

At this point, Captain Doran ended the conversation: "You speak too much English. If you don't keep quiet, I have ways of stopping you up."

The horrors of the passage from Africa flooded through me, and I gave up the fight. My old master took away the one coat I had and left. The nine pounds that I'd managed to save I hid as soon as I was alone.

CHAPTER 7

The Island of Montserrat

WE CROSSED the Atlantic. I stayed on the anchored ship for two months, looking into the lush hills that cupped the plantations on the other side of the surf. The surf was like a terrible, gleaming necklace which bounded the island. Once on the other side of the surf I would be locked in the bright-green, bright-sunned slavery of the West Indies. They unloaded the ship. Then they began loading her again with fresh goods. If I could only stay on board, I would be back in England within three months. The pale light and cold mist of England, which had chilled me so at first, now seemed to feed my daydreams of being free. The ship's holds grew heavier, and I actually thought, yes, the captain will keep me with him. But two days before we were to set sail, the captain rowed out to take me to the island. I pleaded and cried, but he said he knew I would leave him once I got back to England, so he was forced to keep me in Montserrat. More gently, he explained that he'd found the finest master on the island for me, a Quaker who had come from Philadelphia and was known for treating his slaves well. The captain said also that he could have sold me for double the price to his brother-in-law. But he did not want to see me used as an ordinary slave.

Captain Doran was right about Mr. King, my new master. When I was brought to him, he did not tell me what to do. Instead he asked me what I was able to do. I know something of navigation, I answered. I can shave and dress hair pretty well. I can refine wines—I'd often done it aboard ship. I read, write, and know basic arithmetic. He wondered if I knew how to use instruments for measuring weights. When he saw me hesitate, he said that his clerks would teach me if I did not. Mr. King loaded many ships a year. Most of them went to Philadelphia, and he assured me that some day I would go along on one of those voyages. This remark splashed across me like deliciously cold water. Hopes of leaving the West Indies were the only thing that could keep me alive.

Meanwhile, my life hung in suspense among the surfs; my work was to row large canoes to all the different islands. There I gathered rum and sugarcane for my master's ships to take north. With me came other black rowers, owned by different masters. Sometimes there was also a white clerk, because many plantation owners would not trust blacks with their goods. The surf was forever threatening us. Once, passing through the Grenadine Islands, our boat suddenly shot straight up on end, throwing us high on the bank close by. We lay sprawled and stunned under some trees while the boat bounced drunkenly on the ragged rocks. Quick as we were able, we recovered; then we got the boat back, mended her, and tried to set off from the shore. Four times we were lashed backwards. Now what worried us was punishment for not bringing the goods on time—more even than being bruised by the rocks. The fifth time we made it, and rowed hard into the late evening. This happened many times, and as I could not swim, each time I felt close to drowning.

The work was hard. For sixteen hours a day I pulled and guided the boats. Still my master was generous. The other slaves who worked with me were so poorly fed that my master often gave them extra food himself.

Mr. King was the kindest master in the islands. He cared for his slaves well, and if one of them disobeyed or tried to run away, he never whipped him, or even got angry. He simply sold him. As a result, we all served him hard—half because we liked him and half because we didn't want to work for a harsher master. But being a tradesman of sorts, shipping back and forth among the islands, I made friends with other blacks and came to know what they suffered. One friend—an Ibo like myself—was very hard-working. By carefully saving the pennies he made pulling oars, he bought a small boat. The governor of his island, Barbuda, found this out when he was looking for a boat to bring sugar from another part of the island.

So he took my friend's boat—without asking, without paying. My friend went to his master with his complaint and expecting help.

But his master damned him: "What makes you think a Negro has the right to own a boat? If I'd known about your private little skiff, I would have taken it myself!"

Many years later, I heard that the governor had returned to England and died penniless in the King's Bench Prison, while my friend also returned to England—a free and prosperous man.

Another friend was a black Creole. He had been tossed from island to island, and had been branded again and again with the initials of his many owners. He finally ended up in Montserrat. His rare bits of free time he spent fishing off the ragged points of an unused beach. Sometimes he made a good catch; then he would set out for town, where he expected to get a small price for his fish. But every time, some white man would take it from him before he even reached the market.

One day he said to me: "When a white man take away my fish, I go to my master, and he get me my right. And when my master by strength take away my fishes, what can I do? I can't go to anybody to be righted. Then, I must look up to God Mighty in the top for right."

His story made me think how right Moses was in gathering his brothers together and rising up against the Egyptians. And with sadness and pain, I also realized how this man's talk was like the songs we had sung on the passage from Africa.

Stolen fish were not the end of his problems. A little time after he had told me about them, I saw him limping along a road. He had made the mistake of letting a pot boil over in the kitchen. For this, he was beaten so badly that several of his bones had been broken. Later he was sold at the market where slaves are lifted onto scales—as if they were beans or yams—and auctioned off according to weight.

Traveling through the islands, I came to know that the bad treatment my friends got was no different from what happens to all slaves in the West Indies—except only for those that belonged to Mr. King. Even if a white man lost his temper and killed a slave, it meant only a small fine to him. According to the 329th Act of the Assembly of Barbados, "If any [white] man shall out of wantonness, or only of bloody-mindedness, or cruel intention, wilfully kill a negro, or other slave, of his own, he shall pay into the public treasury fifteen pounds sterling." Fifteen pounds! That is what our lives were worth. They make a man a slave, say that his life is worth no more than some trinket they might buy for their wives. Punish him for learning how to trade, forbid him to own any books! Then they say the black man is too stupid to gain knowledge, that his head is as dry and empty as the deserts from which he was taken—ah, but that African land was more fertile than any in all of Europe! My rage grew in those monotonous months of pulling skiffs loaded with sugarcane in and out of the surf. But I was lucky. I had always been protected somehow—by Mr. King, or by some British sailor. Because I did not have to be afraid, I could get angrier and angrier. And soon I knew I would have to find some way to become free again.

But, finally, my desire to be free did not result from the hatred I've been speaking of, but came from the friendships I'd made in England. Even in the islands, I knew an occasional happy mixing of white with black. Once when I was on St. Kitts, a white man with land and slaves in Montserrat wanted to marry a free black woman in the church. The minister told them it was against the law. So the man asked if they might be married on the water, which the priest agreed to do. The lovers went out in one boat, the minister and clerk in another, and, across a sliver of sun-touched water, the minister bent to bless them. After the ceremony, the couple came aboard the ship I was on. We drank to their marriage, then sailed back to Montserrat.

CHAPTER 8

Trading in the Islands

A SLOOP BOAT owned by my master was sailing up to the island of St. Eustatia, and he sent me along to help load the cargo. I carried some fowls and pigs with me, because I knew they sold well on that island. When we landed, a white man came aboard and bought them from me. But the next day he returned, explosive with rage, and demanded his money back. I refused to give it. He began forcing the lock of my chest when an English sailor—not yet rotted by the West Indian climate—saw him and threw him off the boat. That was my first trade.

The sloop was commanded by a Captain Thomas Farmer, who made good money for my master by trading wisely in the other islands. He took a liking to me and had me sail with him whenever Mr. King allowed it. I worked hard, while the white sailors often got so drunk that they cracked the bows of the ships on rocks while trying to slide out of a narrow harbor. Captain Farmer depended on me more and more until finally he refused to sail without me. Mr. King was not happy about this because he had been training me to serve as clerk in his stores. I was called in before them, and was told to make a choice. Much as I cared for Mr. King, I remembered the success of my first trade. Only by sailing and trading could I earn the forty pounds sterling that my freedom would cost.

In St. Eustatia I bought a blue tumbler, or drinking glass, with the three pennies I had. St. Eustatia is a Dutch island, and the tumbler had come across the ocean from the city of Amsterdam. I sold it on Montserrat for six pennies. The next time in St. Eustatia, I bought two tumblers made of a white glass you could almost see through, like thin clouds. On Montserrat, I sold them for twelve cents, or one shilling sterling. On the third trip, I bought two ruby-colored glasses and a jug of a liquor which the Dutch made from crushed grain and juniper berries. They called it gin. All this earned me a dollar on Montserrat!

My friend the fisherman—this was before he was sold—and I bought citrus fruit. We put it into sacks to sell in Santa Cruz (the place I sailed to next). I had two sacks, one filled with limes and the other with oranges. My friend brought one sack of mixed fruits. As soon as we landed, we set out on a chalky road that led to the markets. A fortress ran along the seaside of the road. Its squared rocks were a hardened and cool version of the stuff the soft road was made of. It was very hot, and we slipped into the shadow of the wall as we walked. We went a good mile without saying much. The fruits rolled like jugglers' balls against my back, and I watched my shoes grow white with the dust.

When I looked up, I noticed two figures bobbing like sunspots down the road. Two white men, I saw, as they came closer, and obviously talking about the bundles we were hunched under. They sidestepped to the wall.

"Heavy, aren't they?" one asked, and poked his friend. "Suppose *you* could lift one of those bags?"

The other laughed low in his stomach.

The first grabbed one sack from my back, and I skipped off balance. He passed it to his friend. "How about two?" And taking the second, he tossed it at the feet of the other one, who had his arms wrapped around the first sack as if it were a baby. "Never mind," he continued, "*I'll* try two," and swung the sack out of the fisherman's hands. The white man clowned at trying to balance the two sacks at once, and we laughed at the joke. We laughed a polite bit more, then reached down to take back our bundles. The two men swung them beyond our reach.

"Uh uh . . . you gave us these sweet fruits . . . now don't try . . ." And with our bags, they ducked through an opening in the fort wall and into a house on the other side. We followed, begging for our fruits. They threatened to beat us if we didn't lay off. I continued. We were only just in from Montserrat, I told them, come in on that ship—I pointed. And these limes and oranges were all we owned.

But our being strangers as well as blacks angered them still more. They grabbed for sticks, and we ran. I was still English enough to demand my rights, and went to the commanding officer of the fort with my complaint. All we got were more shouts, and threats of a horse-whipping. My temper was up. Returning their curses in my head, I went back to the house and asked again and again for what belonged to us. It must at last have been as annoying as the drone of a fly, for finally they agreed to return two of the sacks if we'd stop pestering them. As the two were mine, I gave a third of what was in each of them to my friend. We continued into town, and sold them for a fine profit.

I bought and sold and soon had several pounds. Only once did I spend some "freedom money" for a luxury, and that was a Bible. They were hard to come by in the islands. When I finally saw one on St. Kitts, I asked my captain to lend me a few pence—I had brought very little money with me. This he did. He was generally very good to me—defending me when merchants tried to cheat me—and he even gave me lessons in navigation. Some white men got very upset when they heard this. They insisted I would only mutiny when I had learned enough, and navigation was the most dangerous thing you could teach a slave. Captain Farmer listened to them and got jumpy and was gruff with me for a while. But I wouldn't take it,

and threatened not to sail with him unless he continued the lessons. I was taking a chance in speaking
to him like that. But I knew he would be taking an
even greater chance in losing me—I was the only
reliable man he had.

To have a Bible again! My belief in God had kept
me going all these months. Trusting in His goodness
and justice allowed me a blind belief that one day I
would be free. I hadn't forgotten the religious lessons
taught to me in England. I was able to read better
now and there were so many passages I hadn't understood before. But one question continued to trouble
me: why did God tolerate such treatment of black
men? White men left England as men, and after a
few years in the islands turned into monsters. Why?
But I still carried from Africa my belief that what
happens to all of us in our lifetime was decided before we were born. Some black men have become
free. But—this made me anxious—how free were we
even after it was "legal"? The story of a man from
Montserrat rooted in my mind like a nightmare. He
was a free, young, mulatto man, married to a freed
black woman. Everyone in the islands knew about
him and knew he'd been free since childhood—even
the natives of Bermuda knew. But one day the captain of a Bermudian sloop walked up to him and said
he had orders from his master to take him to Bermuda. The man showed him his certificate of birth,
which proved he was free. The captain paid no attention and dragged him closer to shore. The man
asked at least for an interview with the legal sec-

retary or magistrates of the island. Yes, the captain said, but tonight you stay on my ship. And in the middle of the night, the ship set sail. No one heard of the man again.

We pulled into Guadeloupe one day and found the harbor fluttering with a fleet of merchant ships getting ready to return to France. Only they were desperately short of men, we learned when we went ashore. Fifteen to twenty pounds would be paid to anyone who would sail with them. The mate on our sloop and all the white sailors were so excited that they abandoned my captain and joined the French fleet. They wanted me to go with them, and I was tempted. If ever there was a chance to escape, this was it. Freedom and Europe in two months! But up until now I'd been honest with white men. And hadn't my captain shown trust in me by teaching me navigation? If I ran away now, he would never again trust a black man. So I didn't go.

In the late spring of that year, my master traded in the old sloop for one large enough to make trips to America. The new ship was called the *Providence*. As well as cargo, we would be carrying new slaves, because America was growing fast, and the white servants sent there from Europe were not enough to work the expanding plantations. At first, we touched only the sea edge of the city of Charlestown in the colony of South Carolina, and my impression of America remained confused. Tight, fast-moving cities squinched on the edge of an endless, silent land. That

didn't seem to make much sense. I wanted to get to
Philadelphia. Somehow I felt *that* city would explain
it all to me. We returned to Montserrat and learned
that our next trip *was* to be to Philadelphia. Lord, I
was excited! Carefully, I planned what to take that
would sell well there. I questioned everyone for de-
scriptions of the city. In the midst of all this business,
I was called into my master's house. He was there
with the captain.

"I understand," my master said, "that when the
Providence anchors at Philadelphia, you plan to run
away."

I was stunned.

"And therefore," he went on, "I must sell you
again. You cost me a great deal of money—forty
pounds sterling—and it will not do to lose so much.
You are very valuable now. Captain Doran's brother-
in-law would pay a hundred pounds to make you his
overseer."

"Much more than a hundred," Captain Farmer
blurted out, "could I get for him in Carolina. I know
a man right now who wants him to command one of
his rice vessels."

Not being able to tolerate this any longer, I inter-
rupted. Had the captain ever seen the slightest sign
of my attempting to escape, I asked. And if I had
intended to do so, why wouldn't I have gone with the
French fleet that time in Guadeloupe?

At this point, the captain was very silent. After a
minute or so, he admitted that what I said was true.
Besides, he had given me a great deal of freedom in

Charlestown, just so he could watch for signs of rebellion. Surprisingly enough, he'd found none at all.

My master nodded, convinced by the captain's realization of his own mistake. Thank God! I now dared to ask who had told them such lies. It was the first mate, whom I had caught stealing sugarcane from the ship's cargo a few months back. I remembered now that he had muttered through his teeth, "I'll pay you back for this—you're still a slave." I shuddered to think how careless I'd been to ignore his threat. He had almost won.

My master more than made up for his moment of distrust. He gave me some sugar and rum to sell in Philadelphia, and told me the profit on them would be mine to keep. As we parted, he advised me to deal with the Quakers, and then we sailed off. Mr. King was himself a Quaker, I'd heard that, and I knew him to be the kindest master on the island. That Quakers were a type of Christians I also knew—perhaps Christians who were particularly honest. I was more and more curious about Philadelphia.

CHAPTER 9

Philadelphia

DELAWARE BAY NARROWED to a river, and the city of
Philadelphia began its orderly run along the west
bank. The shore was toothed by jutting docks, where
ships waited before their owners' houses like giant
but obedient servants. At empty docks, the dark water
jostled the reflection of bricks and windows. Behind
the shore, a seawall of houses was unbroken except
by sudden shifts in color—from red brick to green
shingles to smooth white with black shutters. The
roofs were low, and rose steeply. But just where the
two sides should have met at a sharp angle, the roof
was sawed off. A flat, narrow walk bounded by white
railings rested on top between two great chimneys.
There the owner of the house would walk im-
patiently, lifting his spyglass to his eye every few
minutes to stare down the river for a first glimpse
of his ship returning home.

If he tilted his head, or swung the spyglass around

too far, he might see a patchwork of gray-green leaves and a cow's rump. For right across the river from Philadelphia were neatly fenced farms, each tree rounded and separate. Growing things never seem to grow out of order in northern countries. Then letting his spyglass drop to his side, he would relax again and watch whatever ship was sailing into port —past Philadelphia's floating windmill spinning and sputtering at the mouth of the harbor, past his own house. I in turn was watching such a man as we sailed in, and when he picked up his glasses a few minutes later, I felt uncomfortable. Would he find a small hole in my pants, or the sweat-spots that faintly shadowed my arms? I turned my back and helped a sailor roll down the sails.

The center of the city was marked by the courthouse dome and Christ Church's high steeple. Two wide streets, High Street and Market Street, ran on either side of the courthouse like canals. The length of Market Street was crossed by covered sheds under which the trading took place. My captain told me how I could recognize the Quakers, and the following morning I went there first thing to sell my sugar and rum. I did find them to be perfectly honest—it was the first time I could trade without tensing, watching, preparing for an ugly argument. After making a very good profit, I walked through the city. I was forever entering mazes of narrow cobblestone streets with slate sidewalks, which eventually emptied into sunlit squares. There were two or three places in town—in front of the statehouse and on the corner of the Merchant's Exchange—where people gathered all day and evening. They talked mainly of politics: colonial laws, taxes, King George of England. These Philadelphians seemed earnest and intellectual people. In Georgia all I heard was talk of crops and stories about slaves.

One thing I overheard that was not about politics was talk of a wise woman who was known for her power to predict things. A man in front of the Exchange was telling a story about her so extraordinary that the crowded listeners kept interrupting him with noises of amazement. I couldn't hear the story, but went back to some shopkeepers I'd met that morning to ask about her. She did exist, they said, and told me where she lived. That night I dreamed of her. It was an ordinary dream, the kind you forget when you wake and remember later in the day only if something reminds you. So, as I made plans to see her that evening—a jingled-jeweled gypsy in bright colors—I remembered with a shock what I'd dreamed. And that in my dream she was not a gypsy at all, but a small woman dressed in the quiet gray of the Quakers. Only her eyes, unblinking as a bird's, were strange.

After work, I quickly went to her house and was speechless when I saw her. She was exactly the same. The very same buttons on her high-throated blouse, the fringe on her shawl was the same cocoa brown. But *she* was not surprised by my startled face and spoke first: "You dreamed of me last night. Come in." We had tea like two ordinary visitors while she related all the things that had happened to me since leaving England. She then told me that I would not be a slave much longer. That within the next eighteen months I would be in great danger two times. But if I escaped both times, everything would go well for me from then on. She blessed me, and I left.

Sunday. Shops and stalls were shut down, the city was quiet. People left their houses grouped in families. The heavy-heeled, heavy-buckled shoes of the grownups rang on the cobblestones while the children scuffed and scraped behind their parents. Families crisscrossed each other as they headed toward different churches. Every few minutes the clack of carriage wheels would get louder, then softer. On the quarter hour, Christ Church bell tolled. It was so high above the city that, no matter how far or near I was, its tone never changed.

All the little hurrying noises hushed at the same time, and the Christ Church bell sounded one last ring that swung in the air like a heavy door swinging shut. I felt foolish in the empty street. All morning I'd planned to go to church; now, suddenly late, I hurried off—then immediately stopped. Where to go? With so many different types, "denominations," I felt confused. This had never been a problem in England, where most people simply went to the "Anglican" church. I had not fully understood the heated talk I'd heard on street corners the day before about the differences between the Quakers and Congregationalists, Methodists and Anglicans. But the fact that there *were* differences seemed very important to the people talking about them, and I decided I should seek out my "native" Anglican church. No, there wasn't time. Down the street, someone had just disappeared into a gray, wood-shingled building—plain as a house and only a little larger. I followed.

Men, women, and children all sat stiff-backed in long neat rows upon wooden benches. Despite the rigid backs and stony faces, there was a strange disorder in this room. I saw no "front," and for a moment had the horrible feeling that perhaps I'd come in the wrong door and was standing under the altar! But no. The other three walls looked like the one behind me. In the middle of the congregation, a woman was standing. She began to speak, in a voice loud and deliberate, yet talking to no one but herself. Looking down but not bent in prayer, she spoke something about the reason for God's existence. I asked a man sitting in front of me who she was. He didn't appear to hear me. The woman continued for a while, then abruptly finished and sat down. I thought, this must be the proper time to ask my question. Again I received no answer, but I saw by a quick creasing on his forehead that he had heard and was annoyed. More people spoke, one after the other from different places in the congregation. Then —silently—everyone got up and left. Outside I learned that these people were Quakers. I tried to ask more about the service, but no one would tell me.

I headed back toward the harbor along side streets, where trimmed bushes spilled over the sides of fences, and the second stories of the houses jutted over the first as if they were sheltering the sidewalk. I couldn't see far ahead of me, and so came very suddenly upon a stone church with people crowded all around. Some pressed in at the door. Some stood on ladders to peer through the tall windows. Some brushed against one another in the churchyard. Never in England or in the West Indies had I seen such a crowd at any church. Someone told me that the Reverend George Whitfield was preaching. I'd heard of him often and was extremely curious. Squeezing my way through the crowd, I managed to get inside. I could see nothing. But the great preacher's voice came to me in strong, rhythmic gusts. And my body swayed to each phrase, as if in response. When the locked shoulders of the congregation would part for a moment, I saw him: a sweat-shining forehead, widespread fingers straining toward us, his body actually leaning into the congregation. He worked the way I had worked pulling boats onto the Montserrat beach. All at once it seemed obvious to me that God's work needed such energy, and I was no longer surprised that the congregations in England and the West Indies were small.

CHAPTER 10

Buying Freedom

CAPTAIN FARMER WANTED to sail the following afternoon. I hadn't counted my savings yet, but knew I had close to the forty pounds sterling that could buy my freedom. That morning I bought a superfine suit of clothes to wear at my freedom dance.

Back in Montserrat, I sold my goods and counted up forty-seven pounds. Forty pounds sterling and seven to spare! The captain told me to approach my master on a certain morning when the two men would be having breakfast together. I came. My stomach tight and knotted to keep me from shaking, I spoke my request. While I was speaking, I listened to my voice as if it were quite separate from myself—a play I was watching in which the main character was someone I wanted to be. I finished. The imaginary play vanished as disappointment and even anger showed in my master's face. My stomach went soft and I indeed began to shake.

"What?" said my master. "Give you your freedom? Where did you get the money—*have* you got the forty pounds?"

"Yes, sir," I answered.

"How did you get it?"

"Very honestly, sir," I said.

Captain Farmer quickly backed me up by describing my dealings in various cities, and my master was silent for a moment. Then he said: "You make money much faster than I do! If I had known that, I wouldn't have given such a rash promise."

The captain jumped up and playfully slapped my master on the back. "Come, Robert, you must let him have his freedom. You laid out your money well and have received good interest for it all this time. Now that it is being paid back, you must accept it. Gustavus will still earn you money—he'll continue to work for you. You know that. Come, Robert, take the money."

My master caught some of the captain's high spirit in spite of himself and said, yes, he'd be as good as his word, and off I must go to the Register Office. I ran as easily as a small child, for at last I regained the freedom I'd possessed only as a child. I loved everything I'd known and not loved before: the hot wind against my eyes, the puff of shoeprints in the dust, the thud of the surf which now was a congratulating drum.

By evening I was a free man. I danced that night in my Philadelphia superfine blue clothes, and the women noticed. Handsome black girls who used to snub me, now stood before me. What splendid proposals I could have made. But my heart was set on returning to London. The next morning, I went aboard my former master's ship. But this time it was as a paid worker, earning thirty-six shillings a month. I was twenty-one years old.

CHAPTER 11

Trouble in Georgia

ONE OF THE first things I learned as a freeman was that many whites would refuse to believe I was free.

Back in Savannah, Georgia, I left our ship tied to the docks, and in a flat boat followed the little rivers inland so I could trade with the people who lived there. The current ran slow, and the shore was spongy with moss. Alligators bred there. The little ones we captured alive, and sold them as pets in Savannah for six cents each. But the full-grown animals were vicious, and I was forced to shoot them, or they would have climbed into our boat. One evening as I was sitting quietly listening for them, the slave of a white merchant came aboard and started insulting me. I asked him to stop. But that only aroused his temper, and he hit me. Enraged, I jumped him, beating him so badly he finally crawled off into the dark. The next morning his master came to the wharf alongside the boat and demanded that I be brought

to town for a public whipping. I answered simply
that his slave had been the first to strike. Captain
Farmer defended me, adding that since I was a freeman, I could not be treated like a slave. But the merchant said he knew nothing about my being "free"—
I was black, and that's all he needed to know. The
town officers would come for me, he said, and I'd be
lucky to get away with just a whipping. After he left,
I was shaking with rage. Never had I been beaten, and
I would rather die first. At any rate, I was going to
stand my ground. But the captain insisted on hiding
me away for a couple of days. Finally I gave in. He
took me to the house of a friend, where I hid in the
attic. Meanwhile, the merchant returned to the boat
with a pack of town officers. After a three-hour search,
they left, with the merchant swearing to get me dead
or alive. The captain then went into town himself,
and spent hours telling the merchant about my
usually good nature. Finally the merchant dismissed
it all with "He can go to hell for all I care." The
captain came for me, and we set out in a hurry down
river for Savannah.

We loaded the ship as fast as we could to make up
for the lost days. Our cargo this trip was mostly
young bulls. They must have felt how impatient we
were to be gone, because as we prodded them up the
gangway, they bellowed and trampled like wild beasts.
One of them turned suddenly on deck and butted
Captain Farmer in the chest—a wound he never recovered from. The captain acted strangely toward
me after that. He had promised to let me take two

bulls of my own on board. But when I did so, he turned on me and said there was no room for my two beasts. I showed my anger by being silent. The captain knew me well enough to read my silence as a sign that I wouldn't sail with him again, and it frightened him. To make up for it, he asked if I didn't want to take some turkeys with me, he'd give me as much room as I needed. This was foolish. Turkeys could never last a long sea voyage, and I told him so. But he kept insisting that I take some. So I did, if only to show I was not angry any more.

It was November, and within two days at sea we were hit by the worst storm I'd ever been in. After eight days, all the young bulls died. We had to pump water from the bilge every fifteen minutes. The captain and the first mate were getting sicker and sicker, and by the tenth day neither of them could move from his cabin. The ship was now completely under my command. Although there was much about navigation I did not yet know, I had learned enough to keep us moving slowly through the storm-ripped ocean, and in the general direction of Montserrat. Seventeen days at sea, and the captain was close to dying. He called me to his bedside and asked me if he had done me any real harm.

"Lord, no!" I said, and, half crying, went on to tell how he was the finest white friend I'd had, that if it weren't for him I wouldn't be a freeman—when I looked at his face and saw he was dead.

The next morning, with the tail end of a hurricane whipping against the sails, we gave Captain Farmer a sea burial. Everyone had loved him, and although the winds calmed in the days following, the air was gloomy about the ship.

The gentle, damp winds that come after a storm shifted so that they were blowing in the direction of Montserrat. This made navigation much easier. With my sails let out far at right angles to the ship, to pocket all the small gusts of wind, I brought the ship safely into Montserrat harbor. Those on land greeted me with mixed exclamations—of sorrow at the death of our captain, and of great surprise that I had commanded the ship. My mates called me captain, and soon all the islanders nicknamed me "the black captain."

CHAPTER 12

Bahamas Shipwreck

I DID NOT want to ship aboard with a new captain, and thought it was time to return to England. But Mr. King pleaded that he couldn't face losing Captain Farmer and me at one time. Wouldn't I make one last trip to America? I felt sorry for him. He was a quiet man, and the captain's death upset him more than I'd at first realized. I agreed to go.

New Year's Day, 1767, the *Nancy* sailed out of Montserrat under the care of her new captain, William Phillips. We carried slaves this time, as well as cargo. Phillips boasted of a new type of navigation which I found very strange: according to the compass, we were on a course four points west of the proper one.

The night of February 4th, I dreamed the ship was wrecked on a circle of rocks. In my dream, the sound of the raging surf was so deafening, I couldn't even hear the voices of men standing next to me. Water soaked through my shoes and licked around my ankles as I stood in my cabin, unable to move. I tried to wake myself up, but fell back into sleep, and the horrible dream continued. Now I was outside the ship in a lifeboat, rowing fainted men to a sandbar.

The following night I dreamed the very same dream.

At dusk on the third evening, it was my turn to work the ship's pump. I was tired and bored, and nearly swore, "Oh, *damn* this ship, anyway!" It was the harmless sort of thing I would have said at any other time, but I remembered my dream, and stopped, sucking in my breath. I went to bed early because I had to get up again for the midnight to 4 A.M. watch on deck. I dreamed the same dream yet again.

The sea was quiet and the night hazy. I paced the deck slowly, listening to the even ticktock of my shoes as they hit the metal deck. At 1:30, the sailor at the wheel called me to come look at a whale he had spotted. I went up and watched it for some time. But when I saw the sea wash against it again and again, I knew it was not a whale but a rock. I woke Phillips, told him of the possible danger we were in, and asked him to come up on deck. He told me not to be foolish. We were on a very safe course, he said, and he went back to sleep. I went back up on deck. By now the wind had dropped off completely—the sails were so limp they slapped gently against the ropes hanging from the masts. Yet we were moving. The current was carrying the ship sideways toward the rock. With no sign of a wind springing up that might fight the pull of the current, I became deeply alarmed. I went down to Phillips and told him what was happening. Still he did not come. The sound of breakers was on all sides now, and the rock only a pistol shot away. I dashed down to Phillips and demanded, what did he mean not coming on deck? The ship is almost against the rock! With that he came. We tried to wheel the ship out of the current, but without wind it was impossible. The only thing to do was to drop the anchor. The surf was now foaming around us. We tied the anchor to a cable—too late. The second it splashed through the water the ship struck against the rock. A terrible scraping sound shuddered through the ship. The surf swelled into great waves, each one curling over the deck and pushing us flatter onto the rock. A sharp prong of rock pierced a hole in the bottom, and the ship began to fill with water. Panicking, I felt my head spin with the memory of past sins. I began to babble prayers.

Phillips meanwhile ordered the crew to nail down the hatches on the holds where the slaves were. Hearing this snapped me out of my panic. Why? I asked. Because they would try to save themselves, and there was room in the lifeboats only for the crew, was the answer I got. I told him that if anyone drowned it should be him for not knowing how to navigate his ship. The hatches were not nailed down. But none of us could leave the ship anyway, because it was dark, and there was no place to go. We settled in for the night, convinced that by daylight most of us would be dead. The other sailors started to drink. Refusing to give up until I *was* dead, I set about fixing the hole in the bottom of the boat with bits of leather and a big clump of candle wax.

When day broke, we were still alive. The tide had turned, taking the higher waves out to sea. Better still, we spotted a small key, or island, about six miles off. But rocks formed a path from our ship to the island, which meant the water was too shallow to sail there. The only thing to do was to row a few people at a time to the island in the lifeboat. The sailors were too drunk to help, which left all the rowing to five of us—three black men, a Dutch Creole, and myself. We worked all day, lifting unconscious men into the boat, rowing, carrying it across rocks, which tore the skin from the bottom of our feet, rowing again. By nightfall, all the men from the ship—including the slaves—were alive on the beach.

On the island, I was a kind of chieftain of the crew. The first thing we saw were some large red creatures coming toward us down the beach. Phillips was certain they were cannibals and wanted to leave immediately for another key about ten miles away. I refused because I didn't think we could save everyone if we made another move. We'd just have to hope they would be more afraid of us, and go away. Suddenly the lot of them spread wings and flapped out above the water. It was the first time I'd seen flamingos.

I had brought limes and lemons on shore. On the other side of the key I found so many turtles and fish that we were able to catch them without any bait. I also spotted a rock in the shape of a punch bowl that held enough rain water to last us many days.

We figured out that we must have been on one of the smaller Bahama Islands. Phillips and I went to work repairing our lifeboat and fitting it with a small sail, and after eleven days, seven of us set out to find help.

On the second day, we came to an island called Abaco, the largest of the Bahama Islands. We had run out of water and were exhausted from rowing in the hot sun. We hauled the boat on shore and went looking for water, but could find none. Thirsty and tired, we made a huge fire to keep off any dangerous beasts, and waited for morning.

The next day, we rowed and rowed but couldn't lose sight of that huge, deserted island. That night we again went on shore, again looked for water. We found a few drops of water on some leaves, which we desperately licked up. That was all.

The third day, we passed several small keys, none of which had water. Our hopes of reaching the town of New Providence vanished. We resigned ourselves to death at last, when Phillips muttered through his dry mouth that he saw a sail. We looked and saw what he had seen, but didn't believe it until we came quite close. It was a small sloop crowded with people. They were friendly—we went on board, but were shocked to find that most of them were in the same situation as we were!

The sloop was a wrecker sent out from New Providence. Its only work was to scout the smaller islands for ships that needed help. The passengers we met on it had had an experience almost exactly like ours: their ship had crashed, and their crew was waiting for help on a small island. The sloop went to our key first. It picked up the twenty-seven men waiting for us, and left some of the "wreckers" on the island to repair our ship and follow us into New Providence.

My seventeen-day holiday in New Providence was marked by long, lazy evenings of good talk with old friends, and much music. Free blacks lived here very comfortably, and they tried to convince me to settle among them. I was tempted, but my longing for England was as strong as ever. So when Phillips had rented a sloop to carry the slaves he hadn't sold in New Providence on to Georgia, I agreed to sail with him.

Scarcely had we left the harbor when a sudden gale blew up and tore most of our sails into rags. A moment later, we were dashed against some rocks. Luckily the water was deep. We managed to get the ship off the rocks and—the boat leaning heavily to one side—made our cockeyed way back to New Providence before she sank altogether.

We got the ship repaired and refitted. My friends swore that someone in Montserrat had laid a curse on us and that I was a fool to go on with this journey. But I was stubborn, and off we went once more. Two months later we reached Georgia.

In Savannah, I came up against the usual disregard for a black man's freedom that North Americans seem to have. One day I was walking on a road quite a ways out of the city. Up ahead of me two white men straddled the road and wouldn't let me pass. One said to the other, "This is the very man we are looking for that you lost, isn't it?"

"The same man, of course—"

I told them both to shut up, because I'd seen their sort of tricks played on other free blacks and they were deeply mistaken if they thought they could get away with such behavior with me. They were startled, and finally one said, "It won't work, his English is too good."

I added: "And my brain is as sharp as my English tongue." They went their way like two scroungy dogs. Such incidents no longer frightened me, but it was good to know I'd never see this savage city again.

Right before I left Georgia a black woman came to me with her dead child. She wanted a church burial for it, but no white man would perform the service. Would I do it for her? I told her I was not a minister and besides, services for the dead did not necessarily save the soul. But she insisted, and I felt moved by the intensity of her wish. Many whites as well as blacks came to the grave—she was greatly respected. I performed the ceremony, then sailed for Montserrat.

CHAPTER 13

Return to Europe

MORE TIME HAD passed since I'd seen Mr. King than I'd even been aware of. We hugged each other, then sat down to talk for many hours. I spoke frankly of Phillips and described the disastrous end of Mr. King's ship, the *Nancy*. Poor man, he had suffered other losses during those months. A pond, or reservoir, on top of a nearby mountain had burst, washing away his house and flooding his crops. I told him again of my desire to return to London. An English ship docked at Montserrat was to leave on her return voyage in three days—I would go with her. He became very sad and tried to persuade me to stay, with promises of land and slaves of my own. I was respected on the island, he said, and people knew me. All this was true, but it was important for me to return to London. I asked him in for a letter of reference. He wrote it as follows:

MONTSERRAT, January 26, 1767

The bearer hereof, Gustavus Vassa, was my slave for upwards of three years, during which he has always behaved himself well, and discharged his duty with honesty and assiduity.

ROBERT KING

I danced my final, celebrating dance on Montserrat the night before we sailed. At 5 A.M., when the beach was still gray but the hills were already green with the first light of morning, the ship began to pull out of Montserrat harbor. It was this hazy gray-green landscape I looked at as we drew farther away from the island. But what I was thinking of was the cruel whippings of female slaves, the instruments of torture that locked their mouths and bound their feet, the terrible surf. I thought of all this and knew I would never return to Montserrat again.

The voyage itself was like a celebration. Fresh winds and clear skies carried us all the way from Montserrat to the mouth of the River Thames in a short seven weeks. I don't know how many times a day I peered at the compass—to see its needle fixed on a point between North and East made me happy all over again.

When we entered the Thames, I pressed against the rail of the ship to watch for familiar landmarks. As we went by low hills and scattered farmhouses, then a village, more villages—they were crowding together now—it all came back to me instantly. I had expected to find England strange after five years of being away, and was almost disappointed that nothing surprised me. But after disappointment came the joy of recognition, when I began to see places I'd actually walked in. The palaces of Greenwich to the left, shipyards on the right, a pub with porches hanging over the river, where I used to drink beer on Saturday afternoons.

Past larger shipyards and merchants' storehouses, we landed at Cherry Garden Dock on the south bank of the Thames and only a mile and a half from London Bridge. We were paid right there on the dock. Never had I made eight pounds so easily in my life! The other sailors disappeared quickly as mice, down streets, behind doors—for most of them had families living in this rough, seamen's section of Southwark town. I was left alone on the dock, free to go anywhere I wanted. For the first time in my life I wasn't obligated to anyone. The next two hours I did nothing but listen to the tide wash against the pilings beneath the dock.

Then I started thinking about my old friends. The Guerin sisters. Were they still living in Westminster? I got a sudden urge to see them, and, shaking off that strange, floating mood of belonging nowhere, I set off through Southwark in the direction of London Bridge.

A fair was going on behind the medieval cathedral. A band of pot-bellied musicians were marching around the square. They were puffing on trumpets and filling bagpipes so full of air that each ballooned instrument nearly knocked over its player. The drummer, as a joke, grabbed a woman who was watching and slipped the strap of his huge drum around her neck. He pushed the sticks into her surprised hands— she blushed, tilted her head, laughed out loud, then started to beat away at the drum while the band marched around her. A tiny dog walked through the legs of beer drinkers—walking on his hind feet and supporting himself with a tiny cane. On the wall of a tavern at the back of the square was pinned a huge painting of a horse with a trap door in its side. The door was snapped open, and out of it an army of miniature soldiers poured. Above the painting it said "The Horse of Troy." Beneath this poster, on a balcony, a troupe of actors was performing a play. They had a clown with them, bending over the railing like a floppy doll and calling for the crowd's attention. In an open bazaar at the far side of the square, I bought a fine blue-and-white china cream pitcher for the Guerins. Not staying to watch the play, I hurried on.

When I came to London Bridge, I was shocked by its bareness. The crumbling shops and houses that made it look more like a cluttered street than a bridge were gone! Now the bridge went across the Thames as flat and bright under the noon light as a country road. I was anxious to get across it and into the familiar streets of the old city.

I went to Ludgate Street first, to the fashionable shops shaded by fringed awnings. There I bought the sort of clothes I had imagined wearing when I used to talk of suddenly showing up and surprising my old friends. Ludgate Street was blocked at one end by St. Paul's Cathedral. Its gold dome met my eyes every time I walked out of a shop, like an impossibly large sun. Then to Westminster. But the Guerins had moved! To Greenwich, I was told. All the way back in the direction I had come from. But with thirty pounds still in my pocket, I hired a carriage and horses, and in two hours I was there. They were so surprised to see me—but just as pleased, I think, as I was to see them. Our friendship took up from where it had left off. The only thing that marked the five-year separation was the adventures I had to tell. They said they had been baffled by my sudden disappearance and were ashamed to hear how their cousin, Captain Pascal, had turned against me that way. But I was no longer angry and even looked forward to seeing him again.

It happened only a few days later. I was walking up the hill in Greenwich Park as he was coming down. He was more shocked than surprised to see me. His first words were, "How did you come back?"

"In a ship," I answered.

"I did not suppose you walked back to London on the water." It was clear that his attitude toward me had not changed. The friendliness I'd expected to greet him with vanished instantly.

"The way you treated me," I informed him, "was hardly in keeping with the way a gentleman treats his most faithful servant."

Without an answer, he continued on his way down the hill.

Not long after this I met him again at the Guerins' house. I asked him for the prize money I had earned during the war and that he never paid me. He said there was none: even if I was supposed to get ten thousand pounds, he had a right to it all. I had been informed otherwise, and said so.

"Well, then," he joked, "bring a law suit against me. Take me to court. There are plenty of lawyers who would gladly support your case. Why not try it?"

"Excellent idea," I agreed, ignoring his sarcasm. Actually I *did* think it a good idea. But the Guerin sisters looked so upset by their cousin's behavior that for their sake I did not want to drag the matter into public light.

Now that I was in London, I had to find work. Perhaps I could be a servant to the Guerins. But our friendship was too close, they felt, for me to "serve" them. They felt I should learn a profession instead. So I settled upon hairdressing, since I already knew something about it. From September to February I was an apprentice to a famous hairdresser in Haymarket. At night I went to school to improve my mathematics. And in the odd hours left over I even learned to play the French horn. When at last I was considered a professional hairdresser, I went to work for a Dr. Charles Irving—a man famous for his experiments in turning seawater into fresh drinking water. Life with him was good. We talked long and often, and he encouraged my plans for educating myself. My salary, however, was poor. This was not the fault of Dr. Irving, who paid as fairly as anyone in London. You simply made more money working aboard ships. When my course in mathematics was finished, I went to sea again.

CHAPTER 14

To Sea Again

I STILL KEPT the sea chest of my old friend Dick who, as I mentioned before, had died in Turkey. Some of the objects in the chest had fascinated and puzzled me for a long time, like a bowl with strange animals painted on the inside. I also found a finely woven rug, very small, with a design obviously meant to be seen from only one direction, as if it were a painting. Dr. Irving and I had talked about this. He guessed it was a prayer-rug—that is, if you are a Moslem, you take off your shoes and kneel on the "bottom" edge of the rug to pray. I developed a great desire to visit Turkey and decided that the next time I went to sea, that country is where I would go.

In May, 1768, I heard of a ship sailing for Italy and Turkey which needed a hairdresser. The captain, whose name was John Jolly, asked me to come to his house and show him my skill. He was pleased with

107

my work, so pleased he signed me up immediately, and, within a few days, we were off.

We briefly touched points of the Italian coast, not staying long enough in one place to get to know the country in any way. But I was left with the luxurious image of pink-stone houses decorated with Greek columns, and of fine wines. We sailed eastward, through the Greek islands. These were very rocky with no trees or fields that I could see. But the rock itself changed colors with the time of day. At noon, an island would be pale purple; right before sunset, shadows colored the hillsides gray-blue and deep purple. In early evening, the same island looked all cocoa-brown.

We anchored at Smyrna, one of the most ancient towns in Turkey, and stayed there for five months. It *looked* like the oldest city I'd ever seen. The houses were built of tough gray stone that was the rock of the earth itself. A cemetery was attached to each house, where generations of one family were buried. The oldness of the city gave me a feeling of peace. I was very happy there. The wine was plentiful, and the fruits—grapes, pomegranates, figs—were sweeter than any I'd tasted. And the people were good to me. They seem to be fond of blacks and actually prefer them to whites. This, certainly, was a new experience for me. An official of the city took such a liking to me that he tried to persuade me to settle there and even offered me two wives. You hardly ever saw women in Turkey, and, when they did come out into the street, they were draped from head to toe in black cloth, and even their faces were veiled. Once in a while, if they were curious enough, they would draw the veil back from one staring eye. That glimpse of startlingly white forehead and an intense eye always fascinated me. But not enough to make me want the responsibilities of a Turkish husband.

During the next three years, I traveled to nearly every country in Europe and visited the magical gardens of Portugal, the marble churches of Genoa, and the bay of Naples, where our ship got covered with black ashes from the volcano of Mount Vesuvius. I even returned once to the West Indies while working for a merchant who traded in Jamaica. I'd never been to Jamaica before and thought it the finest island in the West Indian chain. But the cruelty with which the whites treated the blacks was, if anything, worse than I'd remembered. Yet I was happy—triumphant, even—to see that in the town of Kingston, a large number of blacks kept their African customs. Every Sunday they held a huge dance, where each man danced in the style of his own country. They worshipped their African gods, and alongside their dead they buried the sacred pipes and tobacco that I remember were so important to us when I was a child. Talking to these people brought back memories of Africa that were painfully strong. I wondered again what had happened to my family.

On my return to London, Dr. Irving offered me

my old job again. I needed a rest from the sea. For two years I lived the life of a Londoner, working, and reading Dr. Irving's numberless books. But I could not sit still forever, and soon was off to sea again— this time in the direction of the North Pole.

CHAPTER 15

Arctic Voyage

THE EXPEDITION TO find a northeast passage across
the top of Europe to India was led by a man named
John Phipps. He later became famous for this voyage,
because we sailed farther north than anyone ever
had who came back alive. The ship left in May, 1773,
and in a month reached Greenland. The sun never
set, and it was extremely cold. This continuous daylight was blinding and very *white*. Until then I had
thought of light as yellow and giving off warmth.
Farther north, the ocean became speckled with islands
made of ice, or ice floes, as they are called. Smaller
hunks of ice that looked like round, white cakes
floated light as buoys on the swelling waves. Still excited about finding the northeast passage to India, we
sailed yet farther north. The ice floes grew larger.
They began to overlap, then to pile one on top of
the other, and soon we found ourselves closed in by
jagged mountains of ice. That ice seemed as unmelt-

111

ing as land, and the great Arctic Ocean narrowed to a river running through it. But the air was still clear—above the heaps of ice, we could still see the smoother white line of the mountaintops of Greenland. We continued north. Then one day, clouds of frost-smoke puffed up in front of the ship, and a few hours later we came to a dead stop. Our sea river had suddenly disappeared, leaving us jammed against a bank of ice. We had nowhere to go. So we threw an anchor into the ice, and waited.

Everything on the ground was frozen and unmovable. But the colored patterns thrown against the sky by the Northern Lights were forever appearing and disappearing. The patterns themselves varied so much I never knew what to expect. Sometimes they were rays sparking upward, dancing in the sky like the fireworks I'd seen over the Thames. Or else they looked like silk drapes falling in deep folds over some imaginary palace window. The drapes were green and yellow, with red, ruffled hems. Once we were lucky enough to see the rarest of all patterns—the oval corona, or crown. Its center is pitch black, and flaming out from the center are short brilliant rays that look like rubies, emeralds, sapphires, amethysts.

On days when the wind was still, you could hear the crunch of moving ice floes as they bumped into one another. Or, closer up, the horse neighs of walruses that swam close to the ship. Whenever they came, it was in great numbers, whinnying through their drooping whiskers in a way that made me laugh. After they seemed to satisfy their curiosity about us, they'd swim off again. One day I was rowing up a tiny stream in a long boat with some other sailors when we found a single walrus sunning himself on a floe. We shot him, because we needed food, but only wounded him. He slid over the edge of the floe and sank into the water—probably to die, we thought. To our surprise, he returned a little later, bringing with him a whole "school" of walruses. They attacked our boat viciously and only by whacking their flat snouts with the broad end of the oars did we keep them from turning our boat over. We never managed to kill one walrus during those weeks of waiting. But we did kill a whale or two, and many bears, which kept us from starving.

After a month of waiting for a thaw in the ice, we realized with horror that just the opposite was happening: our ship was actually getting locked in. Moving ice floes had been slowly closing in on all sides until we were trapped in a kind of ice clamp. And that clamp was getting tighter and tighter, which meant that within days the ship would be squeezed to pieces. We sawed away the ice that touched the sides of the ship, to keep her floating in a "pond," at least. Then we hacked away at the ice to the south and dragged the ship through the icy banks like mules dragging a barge along a canal. Over and over, we'd stop, chop at the ice, drag a little, stop, hack away again. After eleven days of this, we were nearly dead with exhaustion, and still no open water was in sight. Most of us knew we would die on that lifeless, moonlike land, and, thinking only of death, we even stopped talking to each other. In this state, I saw my last Northern Light. A shape I hadn't seen before, it was long and narrow, snaking across the sky. Its top or "skin" was a dull silver color, but its underbelly was a brilliant yellow. When the yellow was particularly bright, I heard a faint sound like the lashing of a snake's tail in the grass. Then the light began to fade.

On the thirteenth day, the wind changed to east-northeast. Immediately the weather became mild. The ice bank cracked into many pieces, and they floated out towards the sea. Within thirty hours we ourselves were in open water, and six weeks later we re-entered the mouth of the Thames. Our great relief to be home was mixed with feelings of pride that we had *proved* it was impossible to reach India by a northeast passage.

CHAPTER 16

The Mosquito Shore

MY LAST, LONG voyage away from London was to the Mosquito Shore in Central America, named for Indians who live in Honduras and Nicaragua. My friend Dr. Irving wanted to set up a plantation there and told me that there was no one he would rather have managing his new estate than me. I was flattered, and the new adventure was exciting to me—it would be my first contact with American Indians.

Four Mosquito Indians—three chiefs and a prince —were sailing with us. They had been living in London for a year attending British universities. Mosquitia, as their country was called, had been on very good terms with England for many years, and the Mosquitians wanted to become a British colony. The English, in turn, did not mistreat the Indians the way they did Africans.

The Prince was very young and, though he had been baptized under the Christian name of George, had been taught nothing of Christianity. I was upset by this, and on the trip spent many hours teaching him how to read the Bible and how to pray. He became very enthusiastic—so much so that he'd come to my cabin to pray before every meal. But as soon as the sailors found this out, they made fun of him and teased him with strong liquors. The Prince learned to hate me because of what they said. But at the same time, he disliked their rough drunken behavior. In the end, he talked to no one.

We stopped first at Jamaica. There Dr. Irving and I went aboard a slave ship in from New Guinea to buy slaves for our plantation in Mosquitia. I chose the slaves, and chose all my own countrymen. Six days later, we arrived at the Mosquito Shore. The King came aboard, hugged his son, greeted the three chiefs, and disappeared with all of them into the jungle. We never saw them again.

Sailing close to the shore, we went south looking for the best site for our plantation. At last we settled inland of a large lagoon that was protected from the ocean by an arm of land called Cape Gracias a Dios. Three rivers emptied into the lagoon, and it was along the shores of these rivers that we planted our crops.

The earth was rich, and every kind of vegetable we planted grew quickly. We spent the days enlarging the plantation, and at evening would build huge fires to keep away the wild animals. I never actually saw them, but every night, as soon as it got dark, you could hear in the distance a frightening combination of roarings and howlings. I was told there were jaguars, cougars, parrots, toucans, millions of bats, and many kinds of monkeys. It reminded me of Africa.

After we were really settled in and our plantation was producing food, Indians came to trade with us. Some of these were Woolwow Indians, a people with strangely flat foreheads. They came sixty miles from up the rivers and traded silver for our goods. From our neighbors we got turtle oil and shells, and silk grass. When we needed to build more houses, they would help us—with women and children working alongside the men, just as in Africa. Also, stealing was as great a sin among these people as it had been in my village. We slept under open sheds, and never had to lock up anything valuable.

The Indian Governor of our province was considered a sort of judge: once a year he made his rounds, going from village to village, settling arguments and making laws. Neither Dr. Irving nor I had ever met him; so when we heard that the time for his visit was near, we made careful preparations to welcome him. He sent us his scepter as a sign of his arrival. To show our respect we sent him rum, sugar, and gunpowder. He would be coming escorted by many attendants, we were told, and we expected him to be dignified and majestic. But even before he and his attendants came into sight, we heard a noisy, drunken stampeding through the bushes and shrill cries from our Indian neighbors as they ran to get out of his way. He burst through the trees and stood teetering in front of us. His eyes were wide open and slightly unfocused. His face was flushed. He must have drunk up every bit of the rum we had sent as a gift. We wished to God he had never come, but he was waving his arms madly, filled with himself. There was nothing to do but entertain him. He ate and drank and ate and drank. We just sat there with him, waiting for him to pass out, explode, or run back into the woods. But the food only gave him more energy, and he began hitting our friendly chief and stole the gold-laced hat off his head. This theft was too much for me to take. I had once read that when Christopher Columbus had to put down the Indians in Jamaica, he frightened them with stories of angry gods in the sky. I decided that I would try the same thing. I grabbed the Governor's shoulder with one hand and with the other pointed up to heaven. I told him that God lived there and that he disliked it when people fought the way he was doing. If he did not stop this instant, I went on, I would talk into that book (pointing down to the Bible) and *tell* God to strike him down dead. It worked like magic. He quieted down, accepted a few yams as a farewell gift, and left.

The Indians were so relieved that I had gotten rid of the Governor that they planned a great party in honor of the doctor and myself. Such parties—called *tourrie* in their language—take days to prepare. The liquor they drink comes from roasted pineapples and is complicated to make. The pineapples are squeezed and stamped on by men, women, and children—it looks like a little dance. They pour the juices into a canoe. Then they grind up a kind of tree root called cassava and throw it in with the pineapple juice. If the mixture sits long enough, it ferments and becomes very powerful.

When we arrived at the village for the party, people were already dipping into the large canoe and drinking. Roasted tortoises, ready to eat, were piled high behind the canoe. Beyond these, three live alligators were tied to a tree, their tails whipping in the dust and their heads strained backward, showing the white skin of their throats. I asked what they were there for. To be eaten, I was told. My stomach went queasy. At the base of the tree they had dug a pit, which was filled with burning wood. When the wood burned down to coal, the alligators were cut up, and strips of meat thrown into the roasting pit. It smelled good, I must say, but I couldn't bring myself to taste it.

There was music all night, and the Indians danced. They danced in groups, the men in one, the women in another, just as we had done in my village in Africa. Dr. Irving, who was feeling very merry, got up to join the dancers and innocently went to dance with the women, as was the custom in England. But the women looked so disgusted that the poor man backed off immediately. I couldn't help teasing him.

The oldest man in the province was dressed in a terrifying costume. He wore animal skins with bird feathers glued to them. Great spikes rose from his cap—his head looked like an angry porcupine. He danced his own dance, whooping and imitating the sound of an alligator. The party went on all night, and into the first hours of daylight. I was amazed afterward to realize that all that partying had gone on without one squabble of any kind.

The party had also marked the beginning of the rainy season. We weren't prepared for it. The rivers all overflowed, and many of our crops were washed away. Dr. Irving suffered quite a loss. But not great enough for him to give up, and he had grown fond of living in the tropics, But I was homesick for England. Now, while rains continued and we couldn't work, seemed the perfect time for me to leave. Dr. Irving was very sad to hear I wanted to return and tried a hundred ways to persuade me to stay. But I could not be convinced, and, when a sloop bound for Jamaica anchored twenty miles north of us, I made arrangements to sail. From Jamaica I could easily hop a ship back to England. Just as I left, the doctor put the following note in my hand:

MOSQUITO SHORE, June 15, 1776

The bearer, Gustavus Vassa, has served me several years with strict honesty, sobriety, and fidelity. I can, therefore, with justice recommend him for these qualifications; and indeed in every respect I consider him an excellent servant. I do hereby certify that he always behaved well, and that he is perfectly trustworthy.

CHARLES IRVING

Dr. Irving's letter saved me in the months that followed. The captain of the sloop on which I sailed deceived me. He had no intention of going to Jamaica, but was headed south along the Mosquito Shore. More than that, he claimed that I was a slave, that there was no way a black man could prove himself free. I escaped one night in an Indian canoe. The captain's bullets spraying the water all around me, I arrived safely on shore. After three weeks wandering from village to village, I was able to board another sloop. Again I was lied to and again treated like a slave. But this second captain knew Dr. Irving. When he read the note, he changed his attitude so abruptly it was laughable. But I did finally get to Jamaica. On January 7, 1777, half a year after I had left the Mosquito Shore, I arrived in England.

Since that period, my life has been more uniform and unadventurous than at any time in the years that went before. I shall therefore end my tale here.

EQUIANO spent the next nine years quietly in England. In November, 1786, he was appointed to take charge of supplies for an expedition to settle a colony of free blacks from England at Sierra Leone in West Africa. The idea for the colony started with an Englishman who inherited slaves in the West Indies but did not want to be a slave owner. As the time to sail drew near, many of the black colonists had second thoughts about going. Equiano quarreled with the white organizers. He accused them of stealing money that had been raised for the colony and of mistreating the blacks. He lost the job in March, 1787, and the ships sailed without him. The colony went badly from the start. It was not until 1822 that African colonization succeeded, with the settling of Liberia by freed American slaves.

In 1789, Equiano's book was published. It was a best seller, appearing in many editions in Britain and America. Equiano traveled through England to speak against slavery. On April 7, 1792, Equiano married. It is not known if he had any children. Nor is it known when he died, but it was probably sometime between 1797 and 1811. Although he made several tries—even offering to go as a missionary—he never saw Africa again.

KAREN KENNERLY, who has adapted Equiano's story, is an editor who is compiling a book of fables.